LIFE CHANGE SOLUTIONS

A GUIDE FOR HOPE, HEALTH, AND HAPPINESS

BY

KENDRA CROMPTON

This publication is based on research, evidence-based techniques, experiences, and the opinions and ideas of its author. It is intended to provide helpful and informative material as well as guidelines to assist the reader in finding personal solutions for health and wellbeing. It is sold with the understanding that the author is not rendering medical advice to the reader. The reader should not use the information contained in this book as a substitute for the advice of a licensed health care professional.

Library of Congress Publication Data:

ISBN: 9798666332313

Library of Congress Cataloging-in-Publication Data

Printed in the United States of America 2020

TABLE OF CONTENTS

Part V: Happiness

INTRODUCTION

Are you experiencing a difficult change in your life?
Are you struggling with how to cope, adapt, or accept change?
Have you wanted to make changes in your life, but no matter
how hard you try you just can't seem to?
Have you lost hope that things will ever change?

If you've answered yes to any of these questions, hope,
health, and happiness may elude you as frustration, stress, anxiety, and depression set in and prevent you from moving forward.
I know how this feels. At twenty-six, I was diagnosed with de-
generative disk disease causing me chronic intermittent back and
neck pain for most of my adult life, sometimes rendering me
barely able to walk. I went from doctor to doctor finding little to
no relief. Since then, I've been diagnosed with an autoimmune
disorder, severe allergies, kidney stones, osteoporosis, and rheumatoid arthritis. I know how physical pain can take a toll on both
physical and emotional health.

As for other life changes, I've moved more than twenty times
both in the United State and overseas. I had four children in five
and a half years, the last one on my own in a foreign country with
three little ones at home. As a military wife, I cared for them
alone while my spouse was gone for months at a time, dealing
with children's issues ranging from illnesses, attention deficit
disorder, obsessive compulsive disorder, and addiction. After
twenty-eight years of marriage, I experienced the heartbreak of
divorce. My life changed in what seemed an instant. As I
searched for help to get through that period, I found that doctors

were quick to prescribe antidepressants and anti-anxiety medicines. Therapists listened to me but rarely helped me find solutions. Due to the lack of help I received, I decided to take things into my own hands to find a solution to help myself and other people. At the age of fifty-four, I decided to return to school and get a master's degree in social work.

Having worked as a personal trainer for thirty-six years, I saw the positive effects of fitness and nutrition on physical, mental, and emotional health, but I also saw many who were stuck physically because of mental or emotional issues. I felt there had to be something more I could do to help them.

I researched countless studies on change, happiness, hope, religion, meditation, yoga and Qi Gong. I experienced the benefits of holistic medicine, acupuncture, massage, reflexology, chiropractic, emotional, and energy healing. I studied how nutrition, essential oils, and herbs can heal and treat both physical and mental health. In my studies, I learned and practiced many different evidence-based therapeutic techniques to determine how to best treat mental and emotional health. My goal was to discover the most effective way to help people navigate through the multitude of changes that may occur in life.

Can a pill be the answer?

If medicine were the answer, there would be no need for therapists or life coaches, and you would probably not be reading this. This book is not in any way meant to replace medicine or therapy. I have respect for both and have worked with clients who have found them extremely beneficial. For those currently taking medicine, I recommend consulting your physician before making any changes and understand that the guides in this book can be a supportive supplement to your treatment.

While I've seen the benefits of medicine, there is no doubt we are an overly medicated society. Antidepressants are routinely used worldwide, yet there remains considerable debate about their effectiveness and tolerability. Andrea Cipriani from Oxford University, who led the research on the effectiveness of antidepressants said, *"Antidepressants can be an effective tool to treat major depression, but this does not necessarily mean they should always be the first line of treatment."*

A prime example of this happened to me when I started waking up every morning with racing heart palpitations. I slept well, but each morning upon waking up, the palpitations were so strong I was concerned something was wrong. At one point I thought I might be having a heart attack! I had never experienced anything like this, so I went to my doctor. Within minutes she diagnosed me with anxiety and gave me a prescription for Zanax.

At the time, I was going through a stressful divorce. I was a full-time student trying to navigate school with a huge learning curve. I was working part-time as a fitness instructor and trainer and had just started the required sixteen hour per week internship for my master's program. It didn't take a rocket scientist to see that I might be having anxiety because of my circumstances and that perhaps a life change would help. After going from therapist to therapist, I found one, who gently guided me to cut back a bit, go to school part-time, and put off my internship until the following year. What do you know? My heart palpitations disappeared as my life became more manageable.

3

Medicine has its place, but many doctors are quick to prescribe a pill without considering other options. Research shows that all too often, Americans take prescribed medications that may not work, or that may be inappropriate for their mental health problems. The use of psychotropic drugs by adult Americans increased twenty-two percent from 2001 to 2010, with one in five adults now taking at least one psychotropic medication, according to industry data. In 2010, Americans spent more than $16 billion on antipsychotics, $11 billion on antidepressants and $7 billion for drugs to treat attention-deficit hyperactivity disorder.

Dr. Steven Hollon, a psychology professor at Vanderbilt University, who has conducted extensive research on the effectiveness of antidepressants, reported that at least half of the folks who are being treated with antidepressants aren't benefitting from the active pharmacological effects of the drugs themselves but from a placebo effect. He stated, *"If people knew more, I think they would be a little less likely to go down the medication path . . ."*

So, how do we "know" more? Dr. Amen, one of America's leading psychiatrists and brain experts suggests that instead of guessing a diagnosis from symptoms, we should get a brain scan to know what's going on in the brain. I am on board with this thinking. We wouldn't treat a broken arm without first getting an X-Ray. Why would we treat our mental health without knowing what's going in our brain? While this seems logical, unfortunately this does not happen because insurance companies won't pay for it, and it costs about $1,300 out of pocket.

What are we to do then? I believe both medicine and therapy can be helpful, but they are not magic! The best treatment involves multiple interventions tailored to the needs of the individual. New approaches are popping up all over, with research and evidence suggesting that what is needed is integration of holistic treatment and mind-body techniques to encourage healthy lifestyle changes and to promote overall wellness. This approach can help everyone, those who may need medicine and those who don't.

With this type of approach, I have guided people through addiction, trauma, death of a loved one, loss of a job, divorce, health issues, and other life changes. With all that is going on in our world today, everyone can benefit from healthy lifestyle changes to decrease stress and anxiety and increase happiness in their lives. Whether change is suddenly thrust upon you, or you have a desire to make a change, this book offers alternative solutions to guide you through whatever changes you are struggling with.

PROLOGUE

My own experiences along with many others contribute greatly to this work, as well as research and evidence-based mental health practices and techniques that have been effective with friends and clients.

My years of experience working in the fitness industry have provided me with the knowledge of what works to change one's body, but it is my research and work in the mental health profession, as well as Mind-Body Medicine, that has provided me with insight to mental roadblocks and how we can overcome them.

As a personal trainer, I know what to do to get people in shape, but I wanted to know why one person would succeed while another would not, even though they were doing the equivalent workout and nutritional plan. What I found is that mental, emotional, and spiritual wellbeing all play an essential part in our physical health.

My purpose in writing this book is to give you tools to help you, as well as lift your spirit and lighten your load as you go through change.

Much of what you will find is evidence-based and stems from a solution-focused approach using techniques, skills, and practices in the form of guides to assist you in finding hope and happiness through your journey, no matter how difficult or challenging that change may be.

PART I
CHANGE

"The only constant in life is change."
—*Heraclitus*

CHAPTER 1
UNEXPECTED CHANGE

"It is not the strongest of the species that survive, nor the most intelligent, but the one most responsive to change."
—*Charles Darwin*

From the day we are born to the day we die, our bodies, relationships, environment, and atmosphere change constantly. Some of these changes are wonderful and exciting while others can cause incredible distress and anguish. Our lives can change dramatically in an instant with an injury, accident, illness, or global pandemic. In other cases, we choose to make purposeful change to better ourselves or our circumstances.

Regardless of whether change is suddenly thrust upon us or chosen, it can be one of the most difficult things we experience in life. However, it is the change that stretches us beyond what we feel we are capable of, that often gives us the insight and strength to become who we need to be. We may not like change, but we can respect what we learn from it and what it teaches us.

How we think of change can make all the difference in how it affects us. We can choose to be a victim of it or we can choose to embrace it, valuing the opportunity we have to grow and learn from it. We start by taking one thought, one moment, one step, and one day at a time. By reading this book, you have taken a step toward finding solutions that will help you improve your life and find happiness along the way.

Unexpected catastrophic changes, such as a natural disaster, an accident, a breakup or divorce, or the sudden death of a child or spouse, can seem almost impossible to get through. Experiences like these incur loss, grief, and bereavement which inevitably change the trajectory of our life. They can lead to various struggles like anxiety, depression, identity and personality changes, and difficulty connecting with others. Some people may move forward on their own, but others may need help, as it can often be debilitating to deal with heavy losses. Such changes may necessitate extra support, whether it be individual therapy, group therapy, religious counseling, or friend and family support. Since we are all so different in processing such experiences, the methods for getting through them need to be as diverse as we are. By using a variety of approaches and resources, we have a better chance of finding what works for us.

It is important to understand that while we all go through traumatic change differently, there are some universal stages of grief that we are likely to experience. The following is a brief description of the stages of grief that you may have or are experiencing as you go through changes dealing with loss. I've listed these because having facilitated grief and loss groups, I saw firsthand how easy it is to think something is wrong with us, having never experienced such a range of emotions so dramatically before.

Oftentimes, we feel pressure to get back to "normal" from friends, family, and even ourselves. While we may be familiar with the stages of grief, it can be comforting to remind ourself that these feelings are normal. While everyone is different, most people experience at least some of them and not necessarily in order. Recognizing the stages can help us understand and accept the feelings we may be experiencing.

Stages of Grief

Denial: When we first learn of a loss, it's normal to think, *This isn't happening.* We may feel shocked or numb. This is a temporary way to deal with the rush of overwhelming emotion. It is the brain's way of making sure that we don't get too high a dose of grief before we're ready. It allows us to relax, regroup, and ready ourselves for the difficult feelings we must inevitably face.

Anger: When reality sets in and we are faced with the pain of our loss, we may feel frustrated and helpless. These feelings later turn into anger. We might direct it toward other people, a higher power, or life in general. We might find ourself shouting at people or feeling irritated at everything from minor inconveniences to significant letdowns. This stage can happen at any time, even after we go through a period of acceptance.

Bargaining: When we dwell on what we could've done to prevent the loss. Common thoughts are *"If only…"* and *"What if…"* We may think this is a bad dream and try to strike a deal with a higher power or bargain with God to reverse things.

Depression: When we begin to understand the loss and its effect on our life. We may feel overwhelmed, regretful, lonely, experience sleep issues, and/or a decreased appetite. We may feel sad and cry often and even have unexplained aches and pains. This is situational depression and may pass naturally as we move toward acceptance.

Acceptance: When we accept the reality of our loss. Although we still feel sad, we are able to start moving forward with our life. Complete acceptance brings peace, although we may still have sad feelings at moments, especially at holidays, birthdays, and during death anniversaries.

While we transition through the stages of grief, we do not have to be stuck. Getting back to the way things were may not be possible, practical, or even what's best for us, and coming to terms with that may be the hardest part of the journey. Essential to that journey is accepting our feelings, taking things one step at a time, and having hope that better days will come.

Using a solution-focused approach, people have gone through unimaginable tragedies that seemed impossible to get through, and yet they have done so amazingly well. The outcome of these events can lead to extremely positive life changes - but we have to be open to making that happen. It is even possible to find joy in the journey through change. You may be thinking, *"That's impossible, you don't know what I've gone through or what I am going through."* It may seem impossible, but I assure you, it is possible as you will see from Spencer's story.

Spencer's story

Spencer's life changed in an instant when he lost his wife, Amy, and their unborn child in a car accident, leaving him with four young children. When I asked, how he got through that he said he felt that the hard things he experienced during his growing up years had prepared him.

Spencer grew up with a single mom who struggled with substance abuse but he was determined that his life would be different. He explained *"I looked at the lives of family members with substance abuse, and I didn't want that to be a part of my life. It helped give me the perspective that if I don't want to be like them, then I have to work hard to not turn out like that. I learned to have patience because it was something I could see that my family members didn't have, so I worked hard to have it. Hard things like that helped prepare me for other hard things that came in my life."*

After Amy passed away, grieving alone and being able to function were incredibly difficult, with four little children relying on him for everything, cooking, cleaning, and working. Knowing they were going through something equally as difficult helped Spencer focus on them. There were emotional benefits of being there for them. Serving other people and looking outward were incredibly helpful for him to be able to go on. He said, *"One of the ways we get down on ourselves is when we get overwhelmed and then we see all the problems but if we just focus on the moment it is easier."*

Spencer got support from his family and church, where he attended every Sunday and played basketball once a week. He found that exercise and socializing was good for his physical and emotional health. His faith played a huge role in his being able to get through that period, giving him purpose and hope. He had faith that he would one day be reunited with Amy, which gave him peace, but he was still heartbroken that she was no longer with him. He knew Amy would want him to find another spouse and that his children needed and deserved a mother.

Spencer wanted to find someone who could understand what his children were going through, having lost their mother. He decided to join an online widow support group where he met Erica. At first, they were just friends, but eventually they decided to take the relationship a step further. This brought more challenges, since he lived in Virginia and she lived in Utah, not to mention she had seven children.

Having done many hard things before in his life, Spencer knew he could get through this challenge too. Spencer chose to change his life dramatically. He moved across the country, started a new business and got married. Together with Erica, he finds joy in the adventures of raising eleven children.

Spencer's resilience and ability to get through challenges is not only inspiring but gives us some clear ideas of how we can get through change.

- He recognized his strength to focus on just one thing to do what he had to each day.
- He was grateful to focus on his children, which gave him reason to get up each morning.
- He knew that he had gotten through hard times in the past, which gave him confidence he could get through this challenge.
- He practiced self-care of exercise and socialization by playing basketball and going to church, which was incredibly helpful for his mental, spiritual and physical well-being.
- He joined an online grief group, where he was able to receive the added emotional support he needed.
- He relied on his faith that God was aware of him and his children, which helped him move forward and remarry.

Spencer found peace and happiness amidst this extremely difficult life-changing experience. When we recognize our strengths as Spencer did, we can have the confidence to get through the difficulty of traumatic change and find joy even when it is hard.

Carly and Barbara's stories are two more inspiring examples of this.

Carly's Story

Carly was traveling with her husband to visit their children and grandchildren during the holidays when a semi-truck ran into their car, killing her husband and leaving her incapacitated from the severity of her injuries. Her life changed in an instant. She was laid up in the hospital for many months with a badly broken body. She went from being very physically active, looking forward to growing old together with her husband, to suddenly being alone and barely able to move. She persevered in rehab while being in excruciating pain.

Her mindset was to take it just one day at a time and be grateful for whatever strides she made, no matter how small they were. She has since recovered, after having to learn to walk, talk, and complete basic tasks in a painstakingly slow process. She could have been depressed without a will to live, but she chose to have hope. She continues her journey in life with a newfound appreciation for life, her grandchildren, family, and friends.

Barbara's Story

Barbara saw her life change dramatically when she was diagnosed with multiple sclerosis. She went from being a vibrant healthy college professor to watching her body slowly deteriorate, eventually confining her to a wheelchair. Her organs slowly shut down, and she had to undergo surgery after surgery. After one difficult surgery, she went into a deep depression to the point where she almost ended her life.

Her church community prayed for her, and the women visited her regularly, lifting her spirits and letting her know how much she was loved. Through hope, faith, and the loving support of her husband, family, friends, and church community, Barbara persevered.

After leading a women's meeting one Sunday, Barbara toppled to the floor in excruciating pain. I was struck by how her husband rushed in and lovingly picked her up and gently placed her back in her chair. That love and support has carried her through over fifty years of marriage. Twenty years after that crippling depression, even though Barbara continues to suffer from her condition, she finds joy in spending time with her husband, children and grandchildren, serving in her church and bringing her love and kindness to all who meet her.

Spencer, Carly, and Barbara's experiences show us that the strengths we've developed throughout our lives can help us through the challenges we face, and that love and support of others— whether it's family, friends, support groups or mentors— can carry us through difficult times, and that better times will come.

CHAPTER 2
DESIRED CHANGE

"Your life does not get better by chance,
it gets better by change."—Jim Rohn

Desired changes are those we want in order to better ourselves or our lives in some way. Whether you want to lose weight, quit smoking, stop drinking, or be more patient, kind, or honest, deep-seeded change comes from within. Desired change is an internal process which inspires and motivates us to act. Emotional and mental blocks often prevent us from achieving desired change. Learning to change thought patterns is essential to change. Desired change happens more because of what we think and feel than what we know.

Our thought process is essential to change because thoughts precede action. What you think about most will determine the things you do. For example, how many people know that smoking is bad for them, yet continue to smoke because they are constantly thinking about it? Being able to stop smoking has more to do with what we think and how we feel than what we know.

As personal trainer, I often hear clients say, "I know what I need to do to lose weight." When I bring up nutrition, I almost always hear, "I know what to eat and not to eat." Change doesn't simply happen because we want it to or because we know what to do. Desire and knowledge are not enough to incorporate lasting change. How we think affects how we feel, and those thoughts are directly related to how we change. As you read Nancy's story, consider what thoughts might be preventing you from achieving your desired goals.

Nancy's story

Nancy tried every diet and weight loss plan out there. She was convinced she knew what to eat and only needed to exercise more, so she hired me. I explained that while I was happy to physically train her, she would meet her fitness goals much more rapidly if she followed a few suggestions with her eating habits. She explained she was certain she knew exactly what she needed to eat and not eat and just needed a trainer to motivate her.

We worked within her parameters until slowly she was able open her mind to a new way of thinking about nutrition and exercise. It was challenging for her to let go of what she thought she knew would work and to open her mind to something new. However, once she did, something within her changed, and she was successful in meeting her goals in a matter of months.

"Those that cannot change their mind cannot change anything." —Lao Tzu

Why is change so hard?

"It's only after you've stepped outside your comfort zone that you begin to change, grow, and transform."
—Roy T. Bennett

Change is hard, whether it is sprung on us or because we consciously want to change. Change is hard because we fear what we don't know and are comfortable with what we do. Our human instinct is to do whatever possible to stay safe in our comfort zones, where we know what to expect. Uncertainty brings fear, and the fear of pain is one of the biggest detractors for change. We will do more to avoid pain than to gain pleasure. Subconsciously, the mind works to avoid physical pain as well as emotional, mental, and spiritual pain. Our basic human nature is self-preservation and we will do anything we can to protect ourselves so we cannot just survive but survive comfortably.

When we think about change, it is our human tendency to start to focus on the negative aspect of that change. Our brains are hard-wired with negative bias to more readily register negative stimuli and dwell on them. This negative bias explains why past traumas can have such a long-lingering effect. It also explains why when you start a diet, you seem obsessed with food you can't eat. Evidence suggests this negative bias is likely a result of evolution and man's need to survive by paying attention to dangerous negative life or death threats. Changing the negative bias in our brains to positive is challenging, but research shows it is possible.

By changing the way our brain receives messages, we can change how we feel mentally, emotionally, physically and spiritually. With a positive frame of mind and the right mixture of inspiration and motivation, we can turn things around and stay persistent as we go through change.

It is important to be aware and recognize that our human nature not only resists change itself but also resists pressure from others. Family and friends with good intentions may feel they are encouraging, but it can often feel as though they are pressuring you, which can have the opposite effect on your ability to change.

For example, one newly divorced woman felt she was progressing pretty well, having started a daily exercise program and teaching private art lessons, when she received a call from her daughter who commented, *"Mom, you just need to move on."* This sent the woman spiraling down into a depression again.

While loved ones feel they are being supportive, they can cause you to feel overwhelmed, pressured, uncertain, or guilty. Knowing what stages of change most people go through can be helpful, as we navigate our own personal journey through change.

CHAPTER 3
STAGES OF CHANGE

"Every journey begins with a single step."

Many clients come to me after being told they have or are at risk for a life-threatening medical condition. When their doctor advises them to lose weight to keep it under control or prevent it, they go through stages similar to the stages of grief. Almost everyone admits going through a "denial stage" asking themselves "Is this really true?" Some even get second opinions and then they go through a "mourning stage," asking themselves, *"Why me?"* There is the "acceptance stage," where they admit, *"Yes, this is real."* There is the stage where they must let go of the past and look to the future, the "moving on stage" where they decide they have to do something, and they actually begin to do it. Finally, there is the "Whew, I did it stage," or "I'm at peace stage."

Each stage is independent of the other. Similar to the stages of grief, we may or may not go through all these stages and not necessarily in any particular order.

Stages of Change

Pre-contemplation: "Denial." In this stage we may be aware of the unexpected change or desired change but have no clue what to do or even if we want to do anything at all. This is not a good place to be in for very long, because in the long run it can do more damage and be more hurtful. Looking at positive outcomes of change can often provide motivation for you to move through this stage. This can be challenging as you may not even recognize what that change could possibly look like, so visualization techniques are very beneficial during this stage.

Contemplation: "Why me?" This can be the most frustrating stage of change, as it entails a high level of uncertainty. During this stage many people find themselves unable to accept change or commit to change often feeling stuck as they mentally go back and forth. Staying in this stage too long can cause bitterness and resentment that is detrimental to your spirit and well-being. Examining obstacles such as stress, anxiety, and depression, then identifying ways you can relieve these issues in a healthier way— such as exercise— can be very beneficial.

Preparation: "Acceptance." During this stage we commit to doing something to assist us through the change. We've accepted the change and maybe even begin to take small steps to progress through it. If we are looking to lose weight, we might look up a certain eating or exercise plan or hire a personal trainer. If we are struggling with emotions because of loss, we may look into individual or group therapy. Positive reinforcement from friends and family is beneficial and may help you through the progression of change.

Action: "Moving on." In this stage we put our plans into action and adhere to the plan for at least one to six months. We have made adjustments to our relationships, routines, environments, and ourselves to progress through change. For example, one mother after losing her daughter, changed her routine to walk her dog early every morning. Another man in recovery added weight-lifting to his daily schedule and even set up a gym in his garage to work out when he couldn't get to the gym. It is beneficial in this stage to recognize the positive changes you are making and reflect on what you have gained. Keeping a calendar or journal can be very beneficial.

Maintenance: "I am at peace." This stage is the most important because it is through this stage that we work towards sustaining progress. Once progression has been going for at least six months, you may realize that something you doubted could happen is actually possible. For example, you laugh and smile now. The possibility of going back to negative thought patterns and returning to one of the previous stages is always there. It's important to be kind to yourself and understand that healthy self-reflection well help you continue to progress.

There is no one way to get through change. Everyone is different, so trying different methods, techniques and skills will give you a better chance of finding something that works for you. The following are three well-researched ways to help you through stages of change: 1- Writing, 2- Recognizing Strengths, and 3- Reframing. Consider experimenting with these one at time and then combining them. For example, try the writing exercise for a week or two, then when you feel ready, add the strengths for a time and then the re-framing. Remember to take things one step at a time at your own pace.

WRITING

"The mind is everything. What you think, you become!"
—Buddha

Writing can be an effective way for self-reflection, especially when going through times of change. When we write, we are using our mind and body by physically using a pen and putting down our thoughts and then seeing them as we write and later reading what we've written. It is a great way to keep memories as we often forget specific details in our lives. This is especially beneficial during difficult transitions in our lives when stressful thoughts can be overwhelming. During the challenging times in my life, I found it helpful for me not only to write, thereby releasing preoccupying worries and stress, but also to review past journal entries. This helped me to see more clearly things as they truly were, to avoid repeating the same mistakes, and to look at what worked for use in the future.

Reviewing our life experiences helps us recognize our strengths, talents, and accomplishments, which can help us get through current and future challenges. Writing can help you gain control of your emotions and improve your mental health. It has been shown to be a very effective tool in dealing with stress, anxiety, and depression. Journaling, in particular, is supported by numerous studies to have a variety of therapeutic benefits. One of the top benefits it provides is better sleep, as journaling before bedtime can help release preoccupying thoughts from the mind. Stress and worry at bedtime can stop our bodies from winding down and prevent us from falling asleep. A recent study suggests that writing out your to-do list at night for the next day, will help you fall asleep faster than just writing what happened in your day.

Writing can also help you to be more productive and to accomplish your goals. Writing enables a higher level of thinking, and therefore, more focused action. It can help our brains prioritize what we should focus on and act on at any given moment. Studies show that writing is good for keeping one's grey matter sharp and for influencing positive thoughts. My clients in the fitness industry who write in a food and exercise journal have much more success in meeting their goals in a shorter amount of time than those who do not.

Writing is a very powerful tool to help us through change, not only your own personal writing, but also words of encouragement and comfort from others who are supporting you along this journey. For example, as I write this book, I sometimes find it daunting. However, receiving encouraging emails from my mentor and friends helps me persevere and continue writing. There is something about seeing words versus just hearing them that can make a huge difference. One who is struggling with the death of a loved one may not hear the words of comfort that a friend gives, but when she is sitting quietly alone, she can read them, and feel comfort.

The written word can positively affect a person's progress through change, as we record our feelings and receive encouragement from others. Writing is an extremely beneficial tool to assist people through change, as you will see in the following examples:

At age twenty-one, having only been married for a year and a half with one child and a second on the way, **Erica's** husband was diagnosed with cancer. For the next nine years Erica took care of him and their children. She kept a personal journal and a blog that helped her to express her feelings and process her thoughts. Erica attributes a large part of her ability to cope and find solace to her writing. She said, *"It helped me to tell people how I felt and what I could do to get out of the dark moments. Writing also gave me a purpose. I was able to not only express my feelings, but found my blog helped others. I had gone to a counselor once, but I realized I'm not good at expressing my feelings out loud, so writing things down worked better for me. I would type everything as quickly as I could then go back and read it and then go back and slowly read it again. This helped me process things when I was overwhelmed. It was incredibly helpful to write down at least one good thing, there is always at least one good thing!"*

Writing was very therapeutic for Erica and is for many facing difficult challenges that are sometimes too hard to verbalize. The following are a few more short examples of how writing has helped others, which may inspire you as you begin your journey through change.

Stephanie and Rachel were visibly discouraged as they were admitted to a recovery center. They felt they would never be able to change. After they were guided through a writing activity, their whole demeanor changed. They remarked how much better they felt. Where there had been despair, there was now relief and hope that change was possible.

Kristin was distraught knowing she needed to make a major life change. After trying so many times with no success she felt it was impossible to succeed. When she received a written inspirational quote from a friend, she posted it on her bathroom mirror where she could read it every day. She remarked that this was instrumental in her finally making the necessary change she needed in her life.

David was discouraged and depressed, convinced that his wife would never take him back because of all he had done. He was in a treatment facility and was having a difficult time staying motivated. He had talked about giving up. One day, he received an email from his wife that changed his whole attitude and determination. Because of this one letter, he was able to move forward and they were reunited.

With guided writing assignments, many are able to let go of the past and move forward. Writing is often used in therapy as a technique to help calm and relieve anxiety as well as help come up with solutions to problems. Within this book you will find that many of the guides contain opportunities to express your feelings through writing.

I encourage you to write down your responses in the space provided or in your own personal notebook or journal. Writing is one of the most effective ways we can deal with the challenges of change and it can often make a difference between despair and hope, sickness and health, or sadness and happiness.

GUIDE

Visualize

Take a few moments to visualize what your day will look and feel like once you have gotten through whatever you are experiencing or have accomplished whatever change you wish to make.

Write down specifically what you will do.

For example: "*I will wake up in the morning and make my bed, pray, go for a walk, eat a healthy breakfast of . . . Go to work with a spring in my step and a smile on my face.*"

_____

_____

_____

_____

_____

_____

_____

_____

_____

_____

_____

STRENGTHS

"The secret of change is to focus all of our energy, not on fighting the old, but on building the new."
—*Socrates*

Strengths are defined as traits that are not fixed personality traits, but rather traits that develop from our experiences, environment, and culture. They are what aid us in processing information, communicating with others, and accommodating or making changes in our lives. Looking to our strengths to get us through times of change is essential. Recognizing our strengths will aid in building confidence that we have the ability to get through difficult times of change. You may be thinking, *"I don't have any strengths* or *I don't know what my strengths are."* I promise you do! We all have strengths, but sometimes we can't see them because we are so overwhelmed or distraught. It is important to note that it is not just strength that helps a person overcome adversity, but the belief that the strength can be used to help you through a situation.

One of the biggest challenges we have in life is rising above our own negative self-talk and having the ability to see our strengths, especially when we are going through change. It is the brain/mind negativity bias that stops most people from recognizing their own strengths. The majority of people will focus on their deficits and spend an inordinate amount of time trying to fix their weaknesses rather than building on strengths. This negative thought process inhibits progress through change. Have you ever said, "I can't do this, I don't have the willpower, I'm not strong enough?" When talking with clients about changing their diet, I often hear, "I can't do that."

Alana's Story

Alana was very resistant to change, got mad at me and hung up the phone after screaming, "I can't do that." She called back a couple of days later and said, "You know that book you gave me? I saw the same one on a friend's table when I visited her, and she lost thirty-five pounds. I thought if she can do it, so can I." I often have clients repeat or post signs in their house saying, "I CAN DO IT!" This has inspired many and worked well for Alana. We talked about her strengths and what would help make the changes necessary to DO IT. Some of the strengths she recognized were that she was determined, organized, methodical, energetic, passionate, competitive, strong, and musical. Prior to this, she had exercised for one month with little success, but recognizing and using her strengths helped her with that CAN DO attitude to change her diet, and in two months she lost twenty-five pounds.

One reason we often cannot see our own strengths is that we compare ourselves to others. Social media does not help with that, where everyone looks perfect and posts themselves in their best moment. When you get in the habit of comparing yourself to others, it will put you in a state of consistent discontent.

Everyone has different circumstances in life, and everyone has different strengths that will help them through their journey of life. While others may inspire you to change, the best approach for change is comparison with oneself. Real happiness comes from feeling fulfillment in knowing you have lived your best each day. It does not come from comparing your life to what others posted on social media. When we are tempted to compare ourself to someone else's circumstance, or when something is so challenging that it seems we just can't get through it, all our weaknesses seem to come to the forefront of our mind.

Whether they be connected to an accident, divorce, death, quitting smoking, or losing weight, negative thoughts like, *"I'm not strong enough, I can't do this, I'm not capable"* automatically seem to pop into our heads, causing us to have anxiety and depression. You didn't get this far in life without having some strengths. Recognizing your strengths is essential to combatting those thoughts. One way to do that is to think about past challenges in your life and how you got through them. Some examples of strengths that may come up for you are being adaptable, flexible, resourceful, persistent, disciplined, compassionate, patient, thoughtful, empathetic, intellectual, responsible, etc.

"All that you achieve and all that you fail to achieve is the direct result of your own thoughts."
—James Allen

GUIDE

Write down your strengths that have helped you get through difficulties in the past.

Some examples of strengths that may apply to you are being flexible, resourceful, persistent, disciplined, compassionate, patient, thoughtful, empathetic, intellectual, responsible, etc. Write down as many as you can think of and then add to your list over the next couple of weeks. Notice the tasks that you do competently and ask yourself what strengths you use to do those. If you still can't think of any, ask those closest to you what they see as your strengths, or take an online strengths test.

_____

_____

_____

_____

_____

_____

Think about how those strengths might help you get through whatever change you are experiencing now and write it down.

_____

_____

_____

_____

_____

_____

REFRAME

"Change your thoughts and you change your world."
—Norman Vincent Peale

Our thoughts are just thoughts, and we can decide what we are going to do with those thoughts. We can act on them or not. We can decide to accept our thoughts or let them go, ruminate over them or re-frame them. You may have heard the saying, "Don't believe everything you think." Just remember our thoughts are just that: thoughts. They are our perception of things as we see them based on our memory of the past and information we have accumulated throughout our life.

The voice in our head is our brain and by far the most complex machine on the planet. It computes all our experiences and perceptions and assesses everything to keep us out of danger. Such is the nature of our thought systems. Due to the way our thoughts are wired in our minds, there will always seem to be a logical connection among things we perceive to be true. Our beliefs will always make perfect sense to us.

We react negatively or positively to prove we are right, even if it makes us miserable. Our thoughts can hold us back from happiness or they can bring us happiness depending on what we habitually think about. If we habitually see the negative and are unable to see past our expectations, we will find it difficult to be happy. If on the other hand, we see our thoughts as just thoughts, we can choose to reframe and change them and in turn change our world! We cannot change the past, other people, or sometimes even our circumstances. But, we can change how we think about them.

Too often when people talk about a problem that they want to change, the problem is not theirs to change. For example, you cannot change the death of a loved one, you cannot change your husband, child, mother, or father, and you cannot change illness or injuries. Often the problem is that grief, loss, bitterness, anger, and resentment are causing our inability to move forward and experience joy. It is difficult to change expectations of what we hoped our life would be. That requires us to see the future with a new perspective. What does that look like? It is different for everyone. For some it is changing our view from *"I just want my old life back"* to *"My new life is an opportunity to redefine myself and do what I want to do,* or *life did not turn out the way I expected, but I am stronger, more self-reliant, and have the freedom to do many new and exciting things."* This is called reframing. Reframing is seeing the current situation from a different perspective in order to more constructively move on instead of being stuck.

We cannot change another person's actions toward us. We can only change how we perceive those actions. Many people constantly complain about how their parents, siblings, friends, or spouses mistreated them. They use terms like horrible, narcissists, or talk about how life has been so unfair to them. Inevitably, people will not behave well and life will not turn out as we expected, but it is nothing we can change. What we can change is how we view ourselves. Rather than being a victim, we can reframe our belief in ourselves to be a survivor. Reframing is very effective in helping us change and go through change. The following stories are examples of this.

Krista was sexually abused when she was a child. Her stepmom sex trafficked her between the ages of five and ten years old. She was given drugs and was horrifically abused, but there came a point when she refused the drugs and decided, *"I never want to be like these people."* Instead of becoming a victim, Krista chose to use her strength of conviction to become something different, refusing to turn to drugs or alcohol. She excelled in school, got a college degree, got married, has a family, and now teaches school. She could not change her past, but she reframed her thoughts to positively change her future.

Nali, from India, constantly worried about her life situation, hoping and waiting for someone to help her, until one day she decided to reframe. She changed her worried thoughts from *"What if no one ever comes to help me?"* to *"I have knowledge; I'm physically and mentally fit. I have the strength to find out the ways that I can provide for myself."* So, she did just that, by taking courses on self-reliance and learning as much as she could to improve her situation.

Irene's Story

Irene's world was turned upside down when she was in her early twenties and her husband was diagnosed with Hodgkin's disease. She had been married a couple of years with a toddler and a second child on the way. She was overwhelmed with worry and fear as they were in the middle of building a new house, had no life insurance, and she had no means to support herself if her husband died.

After praying for several weeks, she got an overpowering feeling that she was not alone, and her thoughts changed from *"What am I going to do?"* to *"Whatever I'm required to face, I will be able to do it."* Keeping that in mind, she was able to take things one day at a time and survive. And survive she did! She had three more children, and her husband was by her side to raise them. She felt relieved that crises had been avoided until one day her nineteen-year-old son, Christian, was diagnosed with an inoperable brain tumor.

After a series of treatments and hospitalizations, Christian experienced a stroke which landed him on life support and put her in the very difficult position of having to decide whether to take him off. She thought, *"If he's going to die, don't let me have to decide. I can't let him be in pain and I can't choose to let him die."* She turned to her friends at church and they all prayed together to support her. The next day she and her husband went to the doctors with complete peace, and they knew they could take him off life support. Her thoughts changed from *"I can't do this* to *I know this is the right thing and I don't want my son to suffer."*

She felt her earlier experience with her husband's cancer gave her faith to go through that challenge. Almost as soon as that challenge had passed, her oldest son, BJ, was killed while taking flight lessons. This was such a horrible shock for Irene, but what added to the pain was the suffering of her younger son, Markus who at fifteen years old helped collect BJ's body from the crash.

Markus never got over the mental and emotional trauma of that day and soon took his own life on the back porch of their home while Irene was upstairs. Irene was devastated, feeling like she should have known, and thought nothing she could ever do in the future could compensate for his death. Whenever she would start to have a positive thought, the thought of finding him would come to her head. Then one night she had a dream where she saw Markus laughing and joking and had the overwhelming feeling that he was okay. This helped her change her story from, *"I was a failure as mother"* to *"Markus knows that I love him, and he is in safe place and doesn't have to suffer the way he did."*

A little over a year later, Irene's husband's cancer returned, and he died very quickly. This was harder than any of the other losses because she always had had him by her side. Now she was all alone, but again she reframed her story from *"I'm all alone"* to *"I feel like he's still with me and know he loves me and if I need anything, he will get in touch with me as soon as he can, just like he did when he was alive."* Having her religious faith that there is life after death and that she will be together with Cal and her sons sustains her and gives her hope. When people talk to Irene about them, tears come, but she feels it's a part of love to miss someone, and that's a good thing.

One day her granddaughter had a dream where the stars talked to her and told her she would be with her grandpa again. She said, *"I cried, but it was that 'happy kind of sad.'"* Irene thought that was so profound that when she is feeling sad, she holds on to that quote, *"a happy kind of sad."* How does she get through the days? She keeps busy, painting, writing, and visiting her grandchildren. She turns on her favorite music and dances. *"It makes a difference what story you tell yourself. I have to do some things I don't want to, but you do them and then you start to feel it's okay."*

Changing our thought processes can be challenging, but as you can see through Irene's story, even the most challenging experiences can be reframed, and that can make a difference in how you feel and see the world around you.

Reframing our thoughts takes practice!

Changing our thought processes from negative to positive takes effort, but if you practice every day it will become second nature to you. Studies show it takes sixty-six days to form a habit.

So, start today, right now. Some of you may be thinking, *"Sixty-six days is a long time."* REFRAME to *"Sixty-six days is only two months away to a happier me."*

Recently, a friend shared he had a big blow up with his family and how he could not see things ever changing. He stated that this was a real problem for him and his relationship with his father and he didn't want it to be. Because he was so angry, it was difficult for him to reframe, but he took the challenge to practice. After he reframed, his thoughts and his emotions softened and changed.

Sometimes when we are so emotional about a situation, it takes talking with a friend or therapist to get some ideas of how to reframe, but ultimately it has to be a desire within you that you want things to change. While you cannot change the past or other people, you can change your perspective! This doesn't come by just changing a negative thought to a positive, although that can be a start. It comes from believing the positive is true. So, your reframing statement must be a true statement! The negative will still exist, but it won't affect your life in a negative way anymore because you changed how you see it and how it affects you. Every negative and positive feeling is a direct result of thought. Reframing the thought changes the emotion!

"Change the way you look at things and the things you look at change." —Wayne W. Dye

GUIDE

Every day write down at least one REFRAME! Practice changing your perspective. Write down one negative perspective you can change to a positive. **Examples:**

"I'm stuck at home." **Reframe:** "I am safe in my home and can get a lot of things done."

"I'm all alone." **Reframe:** "I feel good being alone because I can eat beans and not worry about passing gas." (Sometimes silly thoughts make a world of difference. Laughter, even if you make yourself laugh, creates endorphins in your brain and lifts your spirits.)

"My daughter was taken from me." **Reframe:** "My daughter is watching over me and wants me to be happy."

"I hate my step-mom." **Reframe:** "It's good that my dad has someone to grow old with."

"What a terrible time for my cat to die, leaving me all alone during quarantine." **Reframe:** "I'm so fortunate I had the last thirty days in quarantine to be with my cat before she died."

Monday

_____

_____

_____

_____

Tuesday

_____

_____

_____

_____

Wednesday

_____

_____

Thursday

_____

_____

_____

_____

Friday

_____

_____

_____

_____

Saturday

_____

_____

_____

_____

Sunday

_____

_____

_____

_____

"When we are no longer able to change a situation, we are challenged to change ourselves."
—Victor Frankl

PART II
HOPE

CHAPTER 4
HOPE

"Hope is important because it can make the present moment less difficult to bear. If we believe that tomorrow will be better, we can bear a hardship today."
—Thich Nhat Hanh

Hope is believing that good things are possible, that better things will come, and that we are part of a bigger plan than we see today. It is believing that we each have a purpose, however big or small that may be, that our life matters, and that no matter what we are going through there is meaning for it all, and that somehow, some way, we can make a difference. Hope is a necessary ingredient to get through tough times and for meeting everyday goals. Studies have found that hope is correlated with life satisfaction and serves as a buffer against the impact of negative and stressful life events. Hope can exist even with life-threatening health conditions and can lead to better outcomes. In a 2010 cancer study higher levels of hope were found to be significantly associated with lower levels of pain. Pat's story is a perfect example of this.

Pat's Story

At seventy-eight years old, Pat was the epitome of health. She exercised, ate healthy, and was the caretaker of her husband who had recently lost most of his vision. Unexpectedly in a routine doctor's visit, a CT scan showed she had Stage 4B Cancer. She was told it had spread throughout her stomach cavity and was not given much hope for her prognosis. Instead of worrying about what might happen or asking, "Why me?" Pat chose to have hope in her faith in God which has carried her through twenty-one chemo therapy treatments, surgery, clinical trial drugs, and several other attempts to slow the growth of the cancer. Interestingly, she has never had any symptoms of cancer and in spite of everything is active and enjoying life.

She chooses to live each day in a positive way. Every morning she begins her day with a spiritual study. She shows love, interest, and kindness to everyone, even while going through chemotherapy and losing her hair. She is now going through her third round of chemo and continues to be optimistic. When asked how she continues to have hope, she explained that hope is confident expectation. It is possible for her because she has complete trust and belief that God is with her every step of the way.

She credits many writings, devotionals, and scriptures to giving her hope. She quoted her favorite scripture, "Fear not, for I am with you; be not dismayed for I am your God; I will strengthen you, I will help you, I will uphold you with my righteous right hand." Four years after doctors gave her little hope, she continues to live an abundant, happy life, all while supporting those around her.

As you can see from Pat's story, hope can give us the courage to carry on, press forward, and live our best lives. Hope changes our hearts from cynical to believing, from hard to soft, and from sad to happy. Without it, it is easy to fall into sadness and despair. Our very existence is based on hope, the hope that every morning we will wake up.

Hope is one of the key factors for creating change. Hope inspires us to do the impossible and helps us carry on during difficult times. Without hope, people cannot change; they cannot move forward. They often become depressed, turning to substances and even losing the desire to live. Whether going through an unwanted change or desiring a change, we must have, at the very least, an inkling of hope that we can achieve our goals and that life will be better in some way. Whether it's subconscious or in the forefront of our minds, hope is there, and it keeps us going.

According to research, higher levels of hope can predict the following desirable outcomes:

- achievement in all sorts of areas
- freedom from anxiety and depression
- improved social relationships
- improved physical well being

Adrianna's story is a good example of some of these outcomes.

Adrianna's Story

Adrianna had many challenges in her life but always had hope and a CAN-DO spirit, no matter what obstacle came her way. When Adrianna was young, she struggled academically, having difficulty focusing. Socially, she was bullied for her big glasses and homely appearance. This resulted in a daily stomachache, but doctors told her parents nothing was wrong, and she was faking being sick because she didn't want to go to school. This almost cost her life when her parents didn't believe her when she actually had appendicitis. She also suffered from asthma, but when she heard that singing helps with asthma, she joined the school choir, took vocal lessons, and came to love opera. This gave her a vision of one day becoming an opera singer. She hoped to go to college to get a degree in vocal performance. Despite being rejected by her first-choice, Adrianna applied to another university with a very strong opera program and was accepted.

As a nineteen year old student in college, Adrianna decided to enter her first beauty pageant to achieve her dream of both singing and helping young girls. When I met her, she was disappointed she didn't do very well and was deciding whether to enter again the following year. We talked about her talent as an opera singer and how she hoped to inspire others. It was apparent the pageant she entered did not showcase her talent, so instead of giving up hope, she looked into other pageants that might be a better fit for her.

The following year, she entered the Miss Virginia Pageant and though she didn't win, she did very well. This gave her hope to try again. Adrianna had more hope than ever with the loving support of her family and friends behind her to share her talent and her newfound anti-bullying platform. Her hope grew as her vision was becoming a reality. She was excited to share her voice, which had improved over the years, and she was passionate about her anti-bullying platform, seeing how she might help other young girls.

Recognizing that she needed to work on her physique, she asked if I would train her. She had an uphill struggle because of her asthma. She had never exercised regularly before, so cardio work was a real challenge for her. Her first day, she could only do three minutes on a cardio machine and had to stop. She never said, "I can't do this." Instead she said, "Give me a minute and I can get back on." She mentally had to visualize herself doing it before she could physically do it. Once she did that, she went for five minutes, eventually working up to twenty minutes. With each five-minute increment she envisioned herself going that extra five minutes until she was able to do it. She worked extremely hard to get in shape while attending college full-time and managing a clothing store. Even when she was exhausted, she never gave up hope. She made major changes in the way she ate and exercised consistently. In 2006, she won Miss Virginia and went on to sing and speak about anti-bullying in schools all over Virginia.

As Adrianna did, you too can get through your challenges and accomplish your goals by developing hope. I cannot stress enough the importance of hope! We hope that we can get through the day. We hope that the pain will go away. We hope that we can change, or things will change in some way. When obstacles become overwhelming, when challenges become too burdensome to bear, and when pain is so heart-wrenching that we can barely face another day, we may feel as though there is no hope. The good news is there is a solution to even the deepest hopelessness and discouragement you might feel.

CHAPTER 5
WHAT GIVES PEOPLE HOPE?

"We must accept finite disappointment, but never lose infinite hope."
—Martin Luther King Jr

In a survey where people were asked what gives you hope, the number one response was family. Some said, "My mom," "my children," or "my spouse."

The second response was God. Having hope in a higher power who unconditionally loves, is aware and is always there gives comfort, peace and hope to individuals who believe..

Those having both loved ones and faith in a higher power seem to get through change better. This is true for most people whether or not they are religious and no matter what changes they are going through. Knowing that there is someone out there who cares and is there for you, whether that be family, friends, a trainer, or God, gives people hope to press forward and persevere.

Hope may come from hearing another person's experience, such as an inspiring quote or scripture as we saw with Pat. Some people seem to be born with hope and have told me that they are hopeful because. . . *they just are.* For others, hope does not come so easily.

Our hope grows with each challenging experience we successfully get through. Inspirational quotes give me hope. I will often write them on a post-it note and put them on my bathroom mirror, refrigerator, or the side of my bedside table, so I see them when I wake up first thing in the morning. We can find hope in many different ways.

Spencer found hope through his religious faith when he lost his wife and unborn child and was left alone with the daunting responsibility of caring for four young children and still having to work to support them. Amidst his grief, he was able to carry on having the hope that he and his wife would be reunited with their family forever. He believed strongly that God was aware of him and would make everything better until then. This hope along with the support of his new wife and their children continue to carry him through life's challenges.

Bob found hope in his relationships and work. When Bob first saw Phyllis, he knew immediately she was the girl he was going to marry. Once married, they raised two beautiful daughters and owned a thriving dental practice. This was until the day their youngest daughter was diagnosed with Synovial Sarcoma, a rare form of fatal cancer and their life was turned upside down. They closed their practice and moved from Pennsylvania to Florida to be there for their daughter.

Her death was devastating for Phyllis, so much so that she could barely function. Bob knew that this could take a toll on their marriage and could not bear the thought of losing his wife. He said, *"Phyllis meant more to me than anything, and I knew I wanted to spend the rest of my life with her."* Bob decided that if he had to give 100% and Phyllis could give nothing for the rest of their lives, he would do that. Additionally, he set up a new dental practice, which gave him another source of fulfillment and purpose in his life.

He enjoyed his work and spent time with Phyllis until one day he was diagnosed with Lupus Nephritis, a kidney disease which destroys the kidneys. Eventually he had to have a transplant from his only living daughter. Now the tables were turned, and Phyllis had to give 100%. With her constant love and care, Bob recovered, and they are both healthy, exercising daily, eating well, and have been happily married for fifty-one years. Their hope lies in their love for each other and their daughter and grandchildren.

Natalie, who has multiple sclerosis and is confined to a wheelchair, found her faith in both God and her relationships. As her body slowly shut down and she endured surgery after surgery, she became discouraged and depressed. After one major surgery she went into such a deep depression that she wanted to end her life.

During that time, she had the responsibility of being the president of the women's group in her church where she saw to the needs of over a hundred women. Her counselors continuously told her how much she was missed and needed, giving her hope that her life had meaning. Hope and faith along with the loving support of her husband got her through that difficult period. Twenty years later she continues living a life filled with hope. She is happier than she's ever been, enjoying time with her husband, children, and grandchildren.

Kristin found herself once again in a rehabilitation center, after years of struggling with addiction. However, this time she had a beautiful baby boy whom she desperately wanted to care for. Through her discouragement and despair, Kristin held onto the hope she would be reunited with him soon. Her time at the center came with ups and downs. When she questioned her self-worth and ability to get through, therapists and support groups reminded her of her strengths and the person she wanted to be.

She found hope every morning when she looked at the quote, *"I am a daughter of God and He loves me."* She clung to the hope that God was by her side helping her and would see her through so she could raise her son. That hope kept her going and keeps her going now three years later in recovery, raising her son with her partner and a new baby on the way.

Spencer, Bob, Natalie and Kristin all found hope in different ways to help them through the challenges they faced. Spencer found hope through his faith, Bob found it in his love for his wife, Natalie found it through her service in her church, and Kristin found it in an inspiring quote and faith in God. Just as they found hope when going through their challenges, you too can find hope in ways you may never have imagined. Imagining can bring a feeling of hope.

GUIDE

Take a moment and close your eyes, breath and imagine yourself in a beautiful safe place. Notice everything around you. Notice how you feel. Make this a special place just for you. Now imagine a wise guide in any form you like, a person, animal, presence, or perhaps an energy is there to help you and serve you. If you have something you want to ask – advice or a solution to a problem, feel free to ask. This wise person may have a message or gift for you. Take a couple of minutes to spend time with your wise being. When you're ready, say goodbye to your guide and thank them, knowing you can return anytime to this place with your guide. Gradually deepen your breath and open your eyes bringing yourself back to the present.

CHAPTER 6
HOW CAN I HAVE HOPE?

"Hope is being able to see that there is light despite all of the darkness." – Desmond Tutu

You may be feeling you have no hope right now. Many of us get to that point at some time in our lives, but the fact that you are reading this book shows that you have at least an inkling of hope that in some way things can be better for you. Much like the sun is sometimes hidden behind the clouds, hope is often hidden, but it is still there! You have the ability to let hope shine through the clouds. Even those who have lost everything are able to develop hope.

Children in the war-stricken zone of Gaza, who had lost everything including their parents and all their relatives, were able to find hope using mind-body skills.

In his research on post-traumatic stress disorder and depression symptoms using mind-body skills groups, Dr. Gordon saw significant improvements in PTSD and depression symptoms. A decrease in a sense of hopelessness was observed immediately following mind-body skills groups and the improvement remained constant seven months later, despite ongoing violent conflict and economic hardship.

When we feel we can't go on, we hang onto that hidden hope deep inside us, and we muster up the courage to keep going. We just get up and get through one day, or one workout, or one hour, or one minute at a time. Theodore Roosevelt said, *"Courage is not having the strength to go on. It's going on when you don't have the strength."* Every time we get through a moment or day

53

or year, we increase our hope as we reflect on those times we got through. It's a great adaptation as humans that when we get through something it gets easier the next time and the next time after that, increasing our hope for the coming next time. The key is to keep on trying and NEVER GIVE UP!

Dale Carnegie, the author of one of the most famous self-help books ever written said this: *"Most of the important things in the world have been accomplished by people who have kept on trying when there seemed to be no hope at all."*

Mary's Story

After her divorce at twenty-eight years old, *Mary* did not think she had the strength to go on. She had been married a year and a half when she and her husband moved to New York City, far from family and friends. She tried very hard to make things work, and when they didn't, she was devastated. However, with the support of her parents, church community, and a good therapist, she slowly regained her confidence and believed that her situation would improve.

Six months later, Mary met a wonderful young man who fell in love with her, but she was hesitant after all she had been through. She slowly developed a hope that this could work. It took her time but eventually they married. Today they have two beautiful boys and a brand new baby girl.

Many of my clients who have had difficulty achieving their fitness goals held on to the hope that their efforts would pay off. Having a trainer to guide and support them was a key factor to their success. Their hope was strengthened when they had someone in their court guiding, encouraging and cheering them on when they were ready to give up. When we feel we have no hope, having the support of someone else can help boost that hope.

Brian's Story

Brian's weight had fluctuated for the better half of his adult life. At forty years old he was now discouraged, struggling again to lose weight. Finding himself forty pounds overweight, he decided it was time to make a change, but he was uncertain how he could possibly do this with a new job that was emotionally draining and required long hours. He wasn't sure he had the strength to achieve his desired goal.

Using the reframing technique to change his thoughts about food and exercise, he began a different way of eating and living. With guided support and encouragement, he found new hope that he could actually achieve his goal and lost five pounds almost immediately. Brian determined that he liked walking and it was something he wanted to do. Every day, no matter how tired he is, he commits to an evening walk. Face Timing his friends while walking gives him added hope, support, and encouragement. It took him one literal step at a time to develop the hope that he could lose weight and feel better about himself.

Just as Brian continues his journey one step at a time, we can go on and increase our hope one step at a time. The following three guides will help you as you go through change.

Focus on the Present,
Have a Vision
Find Support.

FOCUS ON TODAY

"The secret of health for both mind and body is not to mourn for the past, nor to worry about the future, but to live the present moment wisely and earnestly."
—Buddha

When life changes occur, we can easily lose hope when we live in the past or worry about the future. Too often, we get stuck dwelling in the past, unable to move forward. For example, when a relationship goes awry, many hold ongoing bitterness and resentment towards their ex-partner, ruminating about how badly they were treated. Often this continues to occur for many years, well after a breakup or divorce. It becomes easy to fall into the trap of worrying about the future, possibly ending up alone. Instead of living in the present and enjoying what each day has to offer, we often complain about the past or fret about the future.

Recently, two clients stated that their parents ruined their lives. They claimed that all that has happened in their lives is a result of this and that they would be so much better off if things had been different. This has caused them to spend years feeling anger, resentment, anxiety, stress, and depression -falling into patterns of addiction to numb their feelings.

Ruminating about past hurts and worrying about the future decrease our ability to have hope. We cannot change the past nor can we predict the future. We can only live our best life each day. In addiction recovery there is a saying: "One day at a time." Sometimes it is all we can do to get through one day, one hour, or one minute, and each time we do, it gives us more hope that we can do it again. For example, looking at a course syllabus in the beginning of the school year can be overwhelming, causing

56

anxiety and stress, but focusing on just one assignment at a time, and congratulating yourself for just finishing that one assignment will get you through to the next assignment and then the next, and before you know it, you've gotten through the course. Never let how far you have to go or how hard life has been bring you down to the point where you lose hope.

Look at how far you've come and let that give you hope to lift you up. The key is to give yourself credit for getting through even a moment. Knowing you got through one moment, you can get through the next moment. You can then begin the next moment and congratulate yourself again, enjoying that moment and eventually look forward to getting through each one after that. This certainly doesn't mean neglecting setting goals, but it means doing the best you can each day to accomplish whatever it is you want to or to become whoever it is you want to be. Looking to the future and having something to look forward to is a basic premise of hope, so setting goals and daily priorities is essential. After goals are set, take them one step at a time.

Taking things just one day at time was another way Spencer got through the loss of his wife. He prioritized what he had to do. He got up every day and focused on his four children, made breakfast, got his children to school, did the laundry, cleaned the house, and went to work. This process kept him focused on each day. Once he got through one day, he had more hope that he could get through the next day and eventually things would get better.

During my divorce, sometimes exercising was my only accomplishment for the day, but it gave me hope knowing that I accomplished at least that one thing. Writing a daily list of things you would like to accomplish can be very helpful even if you only accomplish one thing, you can check that one thing off and congratulate yourself for getting it done.

"Yesterday is gone. Tomorrow has not yet come. We have only today. Let us begin." —Mother Theresa

GUIDE

Focus on today by writing a daily to-do list of things you hope to accomplish each day.

Consider writing your list the night before. Studies show this helps you get to sleep faster and be more productive. Don't worry if you don't get everything done. Prioritize and congratulate yourself for what you accomplished. Even accomplishing one or two tasks will give you more hope.

_____

_____

_____

_____

_____

_____

_____

VISION

"Where there is no vision, there is no hope."

—George Washington Carver

When we have hope, we are happier just feeling that there is the possibility of a better future. Having a vision of what that future looks like is essential to hope. If we can see it, we can achieve it. Once we have a clear vision of what we want, we are more apt to achieve it.

Without a vision we have no need for hope, because we don't even know what to hope for. An essential step to develop hope is to have a vision. Spencer had a vision to give his kids what they needed, including a mother.

As a personal trainer I found that when my clients had a clear vision of what they wanted to accomplish, they were able to accomplish it much better than if they just set an arbitrary goal. For example, if you wanted to lose weight, I would first have you visualize exactly what that would be like for you. The vision needs to be detailed. For example, what will you look like? What will you wear? What will you do differently? Visualize yourself exercising, running, walking, biking, or swimming. Where are you doing this? What time of day are you doing it? Visualize yourself eating healthy and nutritious food. What do you see yourself eating? When, where, and what time are you eating? Visualize your healthy breakfast, lunch, and dinner. What will your snack look like?

Adrianna first had to have a vision of herself as Miss Virginia with a sash, being crowned and handed flowers. She visualized herself singing. She visualized herself in a swimsuit and evening gown. She visualized herself answering interview questions with confidence. These all gave her hope, which helped her work hard and accomplish her goal.

A vision helps us sit with confusion and ambivalence while our minds connect the dots and look for creative solutions that keep us moving in the right direction. A vision gives you hope, and research shows that hopeful individuals have greater motivation, persistence, and creativity, because they can withstand the emotional pressure to turn away from pain or uncertainty.

So, what's your vision? It may be a cleaner environment or a more equitable world. It may be something closer to home, within your family, community, or the organization you work in. What's the vision that will keep you striving despite the struggles and the uncertainty you may be facing?

One man and his community found a vision that gave them hope among horrific circumstances. This vision is now making schools safe for children across the nation.

The Parkland Florida school shooting was a horrific tragedy that changed lives forever. It could have left the community in despair, but instead the community joined together to be stronger. Amazing young people stood up and spoke up with energy and enthusiasm that was contagious. Their message was one of hope and a vision for a better future where no child would ever have to be afraid to go to school. That decision inspired the community and the world that we can *"be the change we want to see in the world."* People from every walk of life seemed to be kinder, friendlier and more caring. Even today when you visit that community, you will see signs and symbols posted all over that say MSD STRONG.

Many lives were changed in an instant. Ryan was one of those whose lives changed dramatically that dreadful day. His fourteen-year-old daughter was one of the seventeen students killed on that dreadful Valentine's Day. Fifteen hundred people showed up to her funeral to show their love and support. Ryan mourned his daughter's death and could have rightly wallowed in sorrow and pain for his loss, but he chose to focus on making schools safer for every child. He decided he would do whatever he could to secure the safety of all children in school. He wanted parents to feel safe in sending their children to school. He had a vision that by working with government leaders, laws could be enacted to protect every child.

Ryan worked rapidly with the Florida governor, senators, and the President to institute new safety regulations in schools, and within record time they were passed. Wanting to continue his work, Ryan ran a challenging race for the school board, and although he did not get elected, he did not let this deter him as he continued to work as an activist to ensure school safety. He decided that no matter what, he would work to make change happen to protect all children everywhere. With this sudden traumatic change in Ryan's life, he made a decision to look to the future and use his strengths to help others.

He was recently appointed to be on the Florida Board for the Department of Education, where he continues to fight for a better future for children everywhere. Ryan cannot change the past and bring back his daughter, but her death inspired his vision to make schools safe for all children. This vision gives him and his community hope that their loss will not be in vain and that they can help others never experience the same pain.

Just as with Ryan, we cannot change the past, but we can envision a better future and hope to make a difference.

GUIDE

What's your vision? Drawing guide

(You will need three pieces of paper, which you will number 1, 2 and 3)

1. On the first piece of paper draw a picture of you as you see yourself now.

2. On the second paper draw a picture of your best hope for yourself in the future (Example: getting your dream job, family, travel, being happy etc.).

3. Draw a picture of what you need to do to get there. Example: taking classes, revamping your resume).

Take a few moments to review your drawings and write down any feelings or thoughts you may have.

_____

_____

_____

_____

_____

_____

_____

_____

_____

SUPPORT

"Where there's hope, there's life. It fills us with fresh courage and makes us strong again."

—Anne Frank

Having a supportive network of friends will get you through difficult times and give you hope. Family can be a wonderful support, but not always. And even when they are, it helps to have outside support. It's much easier to find hope within a strong community, as we saw with Parkland.

An excellent place to find supportive relationships is in organized groups, like the widower's support group that Spencer and Erica met in. Support groups bring together people who are going through or have gone through similar experiences and have common ground like cancer, chronic medical conditions, addiction, bereavement, or caregiving. A support group provides an opportunity for people to share personal experiences and feelings, coping strategies, or firsthand information about diseases or treatments.

Having attended and facilitated a variety of different groups, I have seen firsthand how groups can be an effective additional support system. It's very powerful when you see others in a group who have made great strides toward having happier and healthier lives. It shows you that happiness is in fact attainable, which brings renewed hope for the future. Attending a local group is wonderful because you can feel a sense of connection in person as well as meet new friends you can do things with. When that isn't possible, online groups can be very effective. One of my favorite support groups for almost anything is the Mind-Body Medicine group, giving people skills to get through challenging times. This group builds close bonds between the members that often become long-lasting friendships.

You may find groups at a local church. Generally religious communities are very supportive and help in many ways to give you hope and lift your spirits. Besides religious meetings, there are often church-sponsored activities like bible studies, book clubs, exercise classes, quilting, and sports. Members often visit and bring meals when there is illness or death, as well as buoy each other up with spiritual messages and phone calls. Generally, a religious leader is available to turn to for advice, help, and guidance, which can often be just the thing to restore hope when it is lost. Studies found that people who belong to a religious community are significantly healthier and happier than those who don't.

Other options may include online groups or community centers and libraries that have activities where you can meet people with like interests and perhaps find a best friend.

As we saw with Spencer and Erica, who met in a widow's group, there are online groups for almost everything, including divorce, addiction, cancer, grief, and trauma.

When I went through my divorce, I met a new friend at water aerobics. She had been through a divorce and helped me get through mine by giving me a vision of someone who had gone through the same experience. She gave me support, advice and most of all a listening ear. This gave me hope when I was really down. We continue to be close friends years later. Having at least one supportive person you can talk to everyday, whether or not you are going through change, gives you hope and improves your quality of life immensely.

GUIDE

Find support to inspire hope.

1. Think about people you admire whom you can turn to for support. Write down at least three. Talk to at least one of them every day!

   _____

   _____

   _____

   _____

   _____

2. Write down groups or activities where you can meet people with the same interests or experiences. Sign up for and go to at least one per week.

   _____

   _____

   _____

   _____

   _____

   _____

   Look at the attitudes of people around you and see if any of them can serve as role models. Pick at least one and reach out to them.

PART III
MIND-BODY
CONNECTION

Chapter 7
Mind-Body Connection

"The mind and body are not separate units, but one integrated system. How we act and what we think, eat, and feel are all related to our health."—Bernie Siegal MD

Mind-body connection is when our thoughts, feelings, beliefs, and attitudes positively or negatively affect our biological functioning and how our biological functioning affects how we think and feel. Simply put, our mind can affect our body, and our body can affect our mind. For example, have you ever felt butterflies before taking a test? If you have, then you know that the stomach reacts to the brain. Or, have you ever felt your mood lift after going for a walk or run? If so, you know just by moving the body, you can change how you feel. For example, one of my clients suffering from clinical depression found that when she exercised, her mood lifted, and she was much more productive during the day.

The mind and body are closely linked, and their relationship can exert a positive influence on health and quality of life. Emotions ranging from love and compassion to fear and anger can trigger chain reactions that affect blood chemistry, heart rate, and the activity of every cell and organ in the body — from the stomach and digestive tract to the immune system. Emotions can also affect your body's reaction to stresses and strains, which can cause head and backaches and other physical problems.

69

Many psychological therapies make use of the mind-body connection through stress management, support groups, individual psychotherapy, biofeedback, hypnosis, and relaxation techniques. I will be focusing on Mindfulness and Mind-Body Medicine practices to help you get through change. They have successfully been used to help manage stress, anxiety, depression, weight control, substance abuse, chronic pain, fatigue and more. The first step to Mind-Body connection is becoming aware of the sensations of your body. Our five senses play an integral role in our physical and emotional processing. More than 5,000 years ago, the Vedic sages of India understood what quantum physicists are just beginning to recognize: we are all part of an infinite field of intelligence that orchestrates all of the activities in the universe.

With every breath, we exchange our personal energy with the energy of the universe, and we are constantly taking in impressions though our ears, skin, eyes, tongue, and nose. We can develop mind-body connection through several practices to include: breath-work, mindfulness meditation and movement, biofeedback, and progressive relaxation. Many of these practices can be done in your own home, car or office in just a few moments.

Mindfulness

Mindfulness has become very popular as more and more people are stressed from an overload of anxiety with the business of our lives. Once thought to be hokey, mindfulness is now an evidence-based therapeutic method to calm anxiety, stress, and depression. Scientific evidence has found that mindfulness can actually change our brain. Research shows that after practicing mindfulness, the grey matter in your brain's amygdala, a region known for its role in stress, can become smaller. When practicing mindfulness, our thoughts tune into what we're sensing in the present moment rather than rehashing the past or imagining the future.

As we come to accept our thoughts, feelings, bodily sensations, and surrounding environment through a gentle, nurturing lens and no judgment, we can experience more positive perceptions about our lives and the changes we experience.

Mindfulness techniques have been used to manage stress, pain, chronic illness, weight control, substance abuse, and depression. The calming effects of mindfulness can improve our health, helping us experience deeper relaxation, less fatigue, more energy, and enhanced immune system function. I began practicing mindfulness years ago in the form of prayer, meditation and yoga. It was especially helpful in getting me through challenges like moving, raising four children, divorce, and anxiety during my graduate studies.

As a personal trainer I've seen a huge difference implementing mindfulness has had in my clients compared to traditional fitness training without it. By taking just a few minutes before a session to bring thoughts to the body and focus on what we are feeling when we work out, we are able to be mindful of the particular muscles we are working. Clients can actually see and feel the difference in their bodies. Success in meeting fitness goals is much higher once we are able to connect the mind to the body. For example, one man who could barely get through one minute on the elliptical on level one, now, after practicing mindfulness, goes for ten minutes at level seven. Where he once had excruciating back pain, he now rarely has pain as we mindfully stretch during each session. Clients who are looking to lose weight also find much more success with mind-body connection. By incorporating mindful eating, meditation and exercise, they successfully meet their goals and experience overall wellness.

Mind-Body Medicine

Mind-Body Medicine is a practice that focuses on the interaction between the mind and the body by using mindfulness in a powerful way for healing and health. While there are some who may be skeptical of the power we have to heal our own bodies, there is much research that has supported it.

Several well-known individuals are well aware of the mind-body connection and its role in our health. Dr. David Agus, professor of medicine, bestselling author and CBS News contributor said this: *"There's no question that the mind-body connection is real, even if we can't quantify it. Hope is one of the greatest weapons we have to fight disease."*

Another name you may recognize is Tony Robbins, who said, *"While most people believe that drugs heal, studies in the new science of psychoneuroimmunology (the mind-body relationship) have begun to bear out what many others have suspected for centuries: our beliefs about the illness and its treatment play as significant a role, maybe an even more significant role, than the treatment itself."*

Dr. Henry Beecher from Harvard University has done extensive research that clearly demonstrates that we often give credit to a drug, when in reality it's the patient's belief that makes the difference.

While mind-body medicine practices aren't necessarily spiritual, they generally have a spiritual view that helps explore how we are in relationship with ourselves, with others, and with nature and the world around us. Seeing suffering as a universal experience helps us move beyond questioning, *"Why is this happening?"* to *"What might I learn from this experience?"* Mind-body skills groups combine mindfulness with other techniques such as breathing, art, music, movement, and sensory perception. By using both ancient and modern techniques and practices of mind-body medicine, I have seen vast improvements in my own health as well as that of my clients.

The Center for Mind-Body Medicine has done extensive research and used these techniques all over the world to treat PTSD in war-torn countries in the Middle East. A decrease in a sense of hopelessness was observed immediately following mind-body skills groups, and the improvement remained constant seven months later, despite ongoing violent conflict and economic hardship.

I found this to be true with mind-body groups I've worked with as well. The following are a few examples of the positive results.

When **Yadira** first joined our group, she suffered from constant stomach pain that she had for years. Hardly a day went by without her being in pain. After practicing mindfulness techniques for eight weeks, she no longer had any symptoms of stomach pain. She not only no longer experienced pain, but she was able to let go of physical and emotional trauma that she had experienced long ago, accept her feelings, let them go, and move forward in her life. She was desperately seeking the ability to develop a lasting trusting intimate relationship. She reported back to us four weeks after the group ended that while participating in the group, she had met a wonderful man with whom she was now in a serious relationship, and that for the first time she felt comfortable and at peace.

Rhonda suffered from Irritable Bowel Syndrome (IBS) and high blood pressure, which she monitored daily. She joined our group because she was overly stressed due to a new teaching position where she was dealing with misbehaved students, extremely large class sizes, and a demanding supervisor. The job was causing her already high blood pressure to increase even higher. When practicing the mindfulness techniques, she noticed her body felt calmer, she had fewer problems with her IBS, and her blood pressure lowered considerably. By the end of the eight weeks she recognized the need to change jobs, had the confidence to do so, and found a much less stressful job she now enjoys.

Larry, a teenager, joined our group because he was suffering from anxiety from the stresses at school. He often had such bad anxiety from being bullied that he didn't want to go to school. Taking tests brought about stomachaches and headaches that were almost too much for him to bear. After learning the breathing techniques, he reported that he was much better able to deal with the stresses and didn't miss as much school. He particularly liked movement meditation and found this helped with his test anxiety.

As you go through the stress of change, you too can find relief similar to what Rhonda, Yadira and Larry found by practicing the mind-body technique of breath work and mindfulness meditation.

CHAPTER 8
BREATH

"When you own your breath, nobody can steal your peace."
—Unknown

The simple act of breathing is one of the easiest, most funda-mental techniques for present moment awareness. It is the one thing we do automatically, without any thought, yet it is some-thing we can also control. According to many healing traditions, when we breathe in an easy and relaxed way, we create the bal-ance that promotes healing.

In many cultures the breath is associated with the soul or spirit. In fact, in many languages the word for spirit is the same word for breath, and it is understood that there is a fundamental connection between spirit, breath, physical functioning, and physical illness. In traditional Chinese medicine, breathing is also said to be the vehicle for balancing energy in our bodies. Scien-tific studies show that breathing deeply and slowly balances the sympathetic nervous system. When you breathe properly, your muscles relax, and much of the physical tension they hold is re-leased.

Breathing deeply can help us deal with life changes in a healthy and more productive way. Learning to notice your breathing pattern and change it from tension to relaxation is a simple mind-body technique. When we're stressed, we experi-ence a "fight or flight" response. When this occurs, our breathing becomes shallow and rapid. Deep breathing helps to get rid of stress by stimulating the parasympathetic nervous system to induce peace and calmness. This happens because the vagus nerve, which passes through the diaphragm, is part of the parasympathetic nervous system. It wanders up through the belly, through the chest to the central nervous system, and lastly to the brain. It is the part of the autonomic nervous system that brings relaxation. Slow deep breathing slows the heart rate, lowers blood pressure, helps muscles to relax, and quiets the body and mind. Breathing meditations create relaxation in the mind and the body and can be done anywhere at any time with your eyes open or shut.

Just the act of concentrating on your breath takes your focus away from whatever is causing stress or anxiety. Deep breathing can relieve physical pain as well as emotional pain. Most people carry their stress in their neck and back and when they incorporate deep breathing, they often find relief. Focusing your breath when you inhale to whatever area is tense and then concentrating on releasing the tension when you exhale may actually decrease the pain.

When I am stressed, I feel pain in the back of my right shoulder. When I drive in heavy traffic, it starts to tense up. I've found that by bringing breath to that shoulder, inhaling and exhaling deeply and slowly, I have been able to release the tension in that shoulder in a matter of minutes. Deep breathing can also help you sleep better at night. As you take the slow deep breaths, concentrating on the breath versus all the thoughts or worries from whatever you are experiencing, you will find that your mind settles, and your mind and body become more relaxed.

Many people who practice this every night find they sleep much better. Studies done with the Indian Military found on average they fall asleep about sixteen minutes faster when practicing breathing before bed. Deep breathing not only can be relaxing, but it can also bring energy to your body. With deep breaths you inhale more oxygen; more oxygen means more energy. During change, we often find we are emotionally and physically exhausted. Incorporating a short session of deep breathing can help you find the energy you need to get through the day. Starting your day with a short four to five minute breathing meditation can do the trick. I like to begin my day with a short four-minute Qi Gong practice and a Yoga Sun Salutation combining movement with breath work.

There are many other benefits of deep breathing.

- Breathing helps to fuel our bodies, which in turn helps maintain the immune and electrical system and our overall physical health.
- Breathing affects our respiratory, cardiovascular, neurological, gastrointestinal, muscular, and psychic systems. It also has a general effect on our sleep, memory, ability to concentrate, and our energy levels.
- Breathing exercises reduce the workload on the heart by making the lungs more efficient and increasing circulation.
- Deep and slow breaths increase the flow of oxygen traveling through our bloodstream. As a result, more oxygen molecules attach to hemoglobin in our red blood cells. This, in turn, aids our body in the metabolizing of nutrients and vitamins.
- Breathing accounts for an estimated 70% of the way the body releases toxins.
- By focusing on improving our breathing, we can elevate our energy and physical body for optimal health.
- Deep breathing triggers the release of pleasure-inducing neurochemicals in the brain, simultaneously improving feelings of wellbeing while also providing pain relief.

- Deep breathing lowers blood pressure, slows heart rate, improves digestion and improves cardiac function.
- Deep breathing improves our body's ability to bring in oxygen and release carbon dioxide. Increased oxygen flow aids in decision making and the ability to focus.

The Center for Mind-Body Medicine uses a breathing technique called "Soft Belly." It is very effective because when the belly is soft and your abdominal muscles are relaxed, all other muscles begin to relax as well. This breathing method has had amazing results in calming clients when they are going through anxiety and panic attacks.

Mary was one of those clients. She had PTSD from childhood trauma as well as from an abusive marriage and volatile divorce. She was triggered at the slightest stress and would have severe panic attacks with no warning. She had been through years of extensive therapy but continued to suffer from the attacks with little help. When she learned Soft Belly breathing, she finally found a coping skill that worked. She was amazed at the simplicity of it and incredibly grateful to have some relief.

In the mind-body groups I have heard similar comments from all the participants. They are amazed that such a seemingly simple practice can do wonders for their mental and physical well-being. The key is making this practice part of your lifestyle. The more you do it, the better you will get and see the improvements in your life.

GUIDE
Deep Breathing

Take a slow deep breath in through your nose and then exhale slowly out your mouth. If thoughts come, let them go. As you inhale, fill your abdomen with air as if you were inflating a balloon. As you exhale release all the air as if deflating the balloon and relax your abdomen. If thoughts come, let them come and let them go, gently bringing your awareness back to your breath, inhaling and exhaling, relaxing your abdomen. If you feel tension anywhere, imagine the inhale breath going to that area, and the exhale breath taking the tension away with it.

As the tension leaves, bring your attention back to relaxing your abdomen. Repeat several times. You may even want to silently say the word "Soft" as you inhale and "Belly" as you exhale. I suggest repeating this at least six times, but do however many you feel comfortable with. When you're done, slowly bring your attention back and notice how your body feels.

Challenge yourself to do this at least once a day or as many times as you need.

CHAPTER 9
MEDITATION

One way to look at meditation is as a kind of intrapsychic technology that's been developed over thousands of years by traditions that know a lot about the mind/body connection"
—Jon Kabat-Zinn

Have you ever wanted your thoughts to stop for just a moment? Learning how to control our thoughts through meditation can give us the sense of peace we desire.

In today's world with constant change, we think and worry about a myriad of things. When we don't have anything in our life to worry about, we worry about others, our children, siblings, parents, friends, and even pets. Our brain is like a computer with thoughts that sometimes just won't shut down, often causing insomnia and other health issues, until finally we are so overloaded, we crash.

There are many misconceptions about meditation. There is the idea that it has to be done in complete silence or done for a really long time. There are the ideas that it is for religious or spiritual people, or it takes years to get good at. In actuality, there are many different types of meditation, which include mindfulness, guided meditation, movement meditation, mantra, and spiritual meditation. Meditation is the practice of turning your attention away from distracting thoughts toward a single point of reference like the breath, nature, bodily sensations, or compassion. You may be doing meditation and not even realize it.

For example, when going through my divorce, I realized walking was a form of meditation for me. It would help me wind down at the end of the day and sleep better at night. Some other forms you may not have considered are prayer, reading poems, scriptures or repeating a mantra focusing on love, gratitude, or forgiveness. I am partial to moving meditation in the form of Yoga and Qi Gong. A favorite among many clients is the movement meditation of "shaking and dancing." There is no right or wrong way to meditate. Different types of meditation all have value and are beneficial to our health.

Research shows that mindful meditation in particular can have a number of positive benefits, including more positive moods, increased concentration, and more feelings of social connection. Mindful meditation improves a wide range of willpower skills, including attention, focus, stress management, impulse control, and self-awareness. Researchers also found that after only eleven hours of meditation training there were improved changes in the anterior cingulate cortex of the brain, which is a major part that regulates our thoughts, behaviors, and emotions.

In one study, for example, 20 novice meditators participated in a 10-day intensive mindfulness meditation retreat. After the retreat, the meditation group had significantly higher self-reported mindfulness and a decreased negative affect compared with a control group. They also experienced fewer depressive symptoms and less rumination. In addition, evidence also suggests that mindfulness meditation has numerous health benefits, including increased immune functioning.

It is impossible to think about two things at the same time, so training your brain to focus on something other than your problems and worries will relieve that stress at least for the time you are meditating. The following are a few examples of how people incorporated meditation in their daily lives:

As isolation dragged on during the COVID 2020 pandemic quarantine, prescriptions for anti-anxiety drugs spiked 34% in a one-month period. During that time, **Matt** became increasingly anxious and irritable, sometimes lashing out in anger over small things that normally wouldn't have affected him. He decided to start a meditation practice by reading the Bible. As he read, he found he was less anxious and irritable and that little things didn't bother him as much.

After the death of her husband **Irene** found that she would become very melancholy and sad, often crying uncontrollably. She found that turning on some music and dancing was very therapeutic, distracting her thoughts and helping her to feel more positive, even if it was just in that moment.

Michelle found that while going through menopause she had racing thoughts, hot flashes, and insomnia. It was frustrating to lie awake and not be able to sleep, so she decided to try an app with guided meditation. She found it had such a calming effect on her that it decreased her symptoms, and she was able to relax and fall asleep.

GUIDE

Try doing a different meditation each week until you find one that resonates with you.

You may consider trying Shaking and Dancing, which is a favorite in our Mind-body Skills Groups.

Begin by taking a slow deep breath in through your nose and exhale through your mouth. Then, turn on some music with a good beat or rhythm and no lyrics. Start by shaking your hands in front of you, then shake your legs, arms, shoulders, and head. Do this for three to five minutes then stop. Take a deep breath in and out and notice any sensations you feel in your body. Now, turn on your favorite uplifting dance tune and start to sway your body and dance however you feel comfortable. Really get into it, moving your body for another three to five minutes.
Stop and again take a deep breath in and exhale and notice the sensations you feel in your body.

Some other examples you might consider trying include: yoga, prayer, scripture study, guided meditation, or perhaps just being more mindful when eating or walking (you can find a free 10-minute breathing meditation of Qi Gong and Yoga on my website at mylifechangesolutions.com).

"When meditation is mastered, the mind is unwavering like the flame of a candle in a windless place."
—Bhagavad Gita

PART IV
HEALTH

CHAPTER 10
STAYING HEALTHY DURING CHANGE

"The doctor of the future will give no medicine but will involve the patient in proper use of food, fresh air and exercise."
—Thomas Edison

When we experience change, stress levels increase, which changes our digestion and gut health, thus affecting our whole being. Have you ever heard the saying, *"I had a gut feeling."* You actually do have feeling in your gut, the vagus nerve, connects up to the brain which in turn affects your body. For example, you may have a stomachache after you eat, not because of the food you ate, but because you were stressed when you were eating. What we put into our bodies and what we do physically can greatly affect our emotions, mind, focus, and pain. For example, have you ever had a day where you ate all the wrong foods and lay in bed watching TV or movies, then felt lethargic and depressed?

In 2013, I hurt my back so badly I literally couldn't walk. For three weeks I was stuck lying around. So I watched all of the seasons of Downton Abbey, which I have to admit were very entertaining, but my body didn't appreciate it. I felt lethargic, stiff, and puffy all over. I started to get anxious, agitated, and depressed. My body needed to move to get blood flowing to my brain, to lift endorphins and other feel-good hormones. I tried to

89

eat healthy, but chocolate and popcorn were my comfort foods, so that's what I ate. My body was craving movement and nutritious food that could heal it and make it stronger. At that time, I didn't know about healing foods. Since then I have studied and experimented with food, supplements, essential oils, and herbs. You name it, and I've probably tried it. I even became certified as a holistic health consultant. Over the years I've learned a lot about the healing power of food.

There are some specific nutritional guides that can be very beneficial in healing as we experience the stress of change. There's much about nutrition I could share with you, but that would fill another book, possibly two or three, so for the purpose of this book I will focus on what you can do specifically for your health during stressful times. Along with nutrition, we will look at sleep and exercise.

Exercise has been my area of expertise for the past thirty-six years. I've seen trends come and go, and believe me, there are many. Step, kettle balls, kickboxing, Bosu, Medicine balls, Zumba, Cross Fit, HIIT, Yoga, Pilates are just a few of these trends. As with nutrition, I could write a whole book just about exercise, but I'm going to be specific to exercise that will assist you while going through change.

If your desired change is health related, you will find this chapter very valuable. I've researched, documented, and practiced these guidelines myself and with my clients for many years. At fifty-eight years old, I continue to have strong physical health, maintaining my weight and strength to that of when I was in my twenties, exercising vigorously, teaching fitness classing, skiing, and even rollerblading.

Good health has three main components: adequate sleep, good nutrition, and daily exercise. These are essential in balancing our physiological chemistry to combat stress, anxiety, and depression that often occurs with change. As with my clients who have had stress, injuries, cancer, a kidney transplant, paralysis, or those who simply wanted to lose a few pounds, success in meeting physical goals occurs when following these simple guides. You too will find incredible benefits when incorporating these practices in your life.

SLEEP
EAT WELL
EXERCISE
In that order!

I am specific about the order because not only does research support it, in my experience, it works. Often clients come to me with the mindset that exercise is the magic pill that will change their bodies. While I am a huge proponent of exercise and believe our bodies are meant to move every day, I have seen many people who regularly exercise still struggle to achieve their health goals. Our bodies need more than just exercise! You can exercise all you want, but if you go home after working out and eat a half gallon of ice cream, you won't see much change. I use this example because I had a client who did this and wanted to quit training, but her husband called me and told me of her ice cream habit. After agreeing to curb the ice cream habit, she found that she was able to meet her weight loss goal in a matter of weeks.

I had another client who suffered from clinical depression. After working out for just one month, her mood increased, she was smiling again, and she lost twenty-five pounds. Making small changes like changing her sleep habits, curbing her daily intake of three peanut butter and jelly sandwiches, and including regular exercise, she found she had more energy and was less depressed. She went from barely being able to get out of bed and functioning to cleaning her house, cooking healthy meals, and doing fun activities with her children. She continued to consult with her doctor to regulate her medicine, and he was surprised at the positive change.

Studies show that exercise combined with good nutrition and, most importantly, sleep is the necessary combination for good health. Research found that adequate sleep increases muscle mass as much as forty percent. Nine times out of ten, my clients with the most serious health issues, who have the most difficulty maintaining a healthy weight are those who do not get good sleep. Getting the appropriate amount of sleep, nutrition, and exercise will help you remain healthy during stressful times of change.

CHAPTER 11
SLEEP

"The silent sleep loss epidemic is one of the greatest public health challenges we face in the 21ˢᵗ century."
—*Matthew Walker*

Sleep is the most important thing we can do for our health. Sleep is when the body rejuvenates, regenerates, and repairs itself. When we are going through change, our sleep is often the first thing that suffers. We either have trouble falling asleep, getting restful sleep, or even sleeping at all. When we are anxious or have a lot on our minds, it makes it almost impossible to relax and fall asleep. When we don't get enough sleep, we are less patient, easily agitated, more emotional, and we find it harder to function well during the day. The more tired we are, the less we are able to focus at work and at home. This leads to even more stress, making it likelier to snap at family and friends, which causes us more stress. This can have long term negative impacts on our relationships and our physical well-being. Lack of sleep increases the risk for obesity, heart disease, and infections.

Our body releases hormones during sleep that help repair cells and control the body's use of energy. These hormone changes can affect body weight. This is apparent with my personal training clients. Those who have the most difficult time losing weight are those who get under six hours of sleep. When we are sleep deprived, we create stress in our body, which then goes into survival mode, holding onto fat and making it almost impossible to maintain a healthy weight. The good news is that by increasing our sleep, we can increase our muscle mass by as much as forty percent, reduce body fat, strengthen our brain, and decrease stress hormones. Paul's experience is a great example of this.

Paul had profound positive health changes after he retired from the military. He credits this to getting eight hours of sleep in comparison to the six hours of sleep he got while working. Within one month he lost fifteen pounds without doing anything different, except sleeping more. His anxiety went down, his IBS subsided, his mind was clearer, and he could focus better.

In his book, *Why We Sleep*, neuroscientist Mathew Walker states, *"A balanced diet and exercise are of vital importance, but we now see sleep as the preeminent force in this health trinity. The physical and mental impairment caused by one night of bad sleep dwarf those caused by an equivalent absence of food or exercise... Sleep is the single most effective thing we can do to reset our brain and body health each day."*

When and how much sleep should we get?

While everyone has different sleep requirements, most adults need seven to nine hours of sleep. Our natural sleep/wake cycles are very much in tune with the sun and our environment. The cycles of light and dark that result from the movement of the sun and planets affect nearly all living things, especially humans. This is a term we call the circadian rhythm and it is like our time-keeping clock.

Circadian rhythm affects our brain, body, and hormones, helping us stay awake and telling our body when it's time to sleep. In response to the light, your hormonal system naturally releases cortisol, and cortisol levels begin dropping as the sun goes down in the afternoon. Sunlight also increases the brain's release of the hormone serotonin, which lifts mood and helps us feel calm and focused. At night, darker lighting triggers the brain to make the hormone melatonin, which helps you sleep and increases the levels of growth and repair hormones.

Your circadian rhythm works best when you have regular sleep habits, like going to bed at night and waking up in the morning around the same times from day to day. Our bodies are designed to wind down from sunset until about 10:00pm when sleep and physical repair should begin and takes place predominantly from about 2:00am to 6:00am. Studies show that the pineal gland secretes melatonin between 10:00pm and 200am, and we miss the window of cellular repair time when we stay up too late. Scientists as well as Qi Gong professionals recommend going to bed between 10:00 and 11:00pm and rising between 6:00 and 7:00am to balance your body chemistry and Qi.

Why we can't sleep

Worry, anxiety, stress, and depression are the most common reasons why we can't sleep. Other common emotional and psychological causes include anger, grief, bipolar disorder, and trauma. Medical conditions and diseases such as asthma, allergies, acid reflux, and chronic pain can also inhibit our sleep. Many of the medications we take can interfere with sleep including antidepressants, stimulants for ADHD, thyroid medications, high blood pressure medications, and even some contraceptives. Pain relief medications that contain caffeine such as Midol and Excedrin can also keep us awake.

Other habits we don't think about can negatively impact our ability to sleep like napping, eating sugary foods or heavy meals too close to bedtime, and not getting enough exercise or exercising too late in the day. Not only can poor daytime habits contribute to insomnia, but a poor night's sleep can make these habits harder to correct. More often than not, we have difficulty sleeping because we can't shut our mind off from thinking, especially when we are going through change.

Our brain is like a computer trying to solve a problem. It won't shut down until it is resolved or we signal it to shut down. The more trouble we have with sleep, the more it starts to invade our thoughts. You may start to dread going to sleep because you just know that you're going to toss and turn for hours, wake up at 2:00am again, or stress about how you need sleep so you can be productive the next day. Worrying about getting to sleep or thinking about how tired we're going to be floods our body with adrenaline, and before we know it, we're wide awake.

Change such as the 2020 pandemic quarantine caused a marked increase in sleep problems and anxiety. The use of anti-insomnia, anti-anxiety, and antidepressant medications spiked, with filled prescriptions increasing by 21% in one month. When we're frustrated with the inability to sleep it may seem like the only alternative is to turn to prescription sleep medications.

According to the CDC, over nine million Americans use prescription sleep aids. These can actually disrupt sleep even more over the long-term. Before trying a sleep aid prescription, consider trying some or all of the following tips:

- Write. Write in gratitude journal. Keep a journal near your bed to write down any thoughts that may come up. Write your to-do list for the next day. This allows the mind to relax and frees it from worry and stress.
- Take a hot bath with Epsom salts. It will drop your body temperature, signaling to the body that it's time to sleep. The magnesium in the Epsom salts decrease inflammation and may also help your body produce melatonin.
- Go to bed and wake up at the same time every day. Your body's circadian rhythm functions on a set loop, aligning itself with sunrise and sunset.
- Keep your bedroom temperature around 70 degrees Fahrenheit for optimal cooling of your body during sleep. Wear socks if your feet are cold.
- Avoid caffeine after 1:00pm and avoid alcohol. It blocks your REM sleep, an important part of the sleep cycle.
- An hour before bedtime, dim the lights and turn off all screens, especially computers and phones that have the highest amount of blue light.
- Drink an herbal tea like cinnamon, peppermint, lavender, licorice, or chamomile.

- Avoid taking a nap during the day. It confuses your internal clock. If you have to nap, keep it to thirty minutes before 3:00pm.
- Go for a morning walk outside. Studies found that daytime bright light exposure improved sleep quality and duration and reduced the time it took to fall asleep by 83%. In older adults, two hours of bright light exposure during the day increased the amount of sleep by two hours.
- Don't eat too late in the evening. Eating a large meal before bed can lead to poor sleep and hormone disruption.
- Have a pre-sleep relaxing routine such as meditating, prayer, reading, music, etc. This lets your mind and body know it's time to sleep.
- Try listening to an audio meditation or a calming app such as Calm, Breath or Headspace.
- Practice deep breathing, slowly and deeply inhaling through your nose, and exhaling through your mouth while softening the abdominal cage.
- Daily exercise has been scientifically proven to improve all aspects of sleep and health. In people with severe insomnia, exercise offered more benefits than most drugs. Exercise reduced time to fall asleep by 55%, total night wakefulness by 30%, and anxiety by 15%.

GUIDE

Sleep Routine

Prepare for bed at least one hour before you go to sleep by using one or more of the tips to create a personal bedtime routine.

-Exercise daily– even if it's just a twenty to thirty-minute walk.

-Set a goal of getting at least seven hours of sleep nightly and aim to get to sleep before 11:00pm.

-Keep a record of how you feel.

M   -

_____

T_____

_____

W_____

_____

TH_____

_____

F_____

_____

S_____

_____

SU_____

_____

CHAPTER 12
NUTRITION

"All of us have the power to heal ourselves."
—*Hippocrates*

Nutrition affects us more than we may realize. Often, we are so concerned with how food affects us physically, we don't realize how it affects us mentally and emotionally. For example, after you've eaten a large meal at a restaurant, you may feel tired, bloated, and gassy, not recognizing that you are also irritable and impatient because of what you ate. The opposite is true as well. Often times after we eat, we have a stomachache not because of what we've eaten but because of an argument we had just before eating, causing internal stress.

The direct relationship of our brain to our gut causes our gastrointestinal system to be sensitive to emotions and reactions such as stress. When we are stressed, our brain sends signals to release chemicals such as cortisol, adrenaline, and serotonin. Serotonin is a neurotransmitter that helps regulate sleep and appetite, regulates moods, and inhibits pain. Ninety-five percent of your serotonin is produced in your gastrointestinal tract.

When we are stressed, these chemicals can cause adverse reactions and negatively affect our digestive system in many ways, causing a decrease in blood and oxygen flow to the stomach, cramping, an imbalance in gut bacteria, and inflammation. These symptoms can develop into gastrointestinal disorders such as irritable bowel syndrome, peptic ulcers, and acid reflux. The good news is that we can alleviate stress, anxiety and depression, and actually heal our body by what we put in it.

Susan is a great example of this. She was in her late fifties when she first began attending an exercise and nutrition class. She had breast cancer several years prior and had been exercising and eating healthy for about ten years when the cancer returned. She shared this experience: *"The first time I had cancer I didn't exercise or eat very well. After surgery and chemotherapy my pain and recovery time were so much worse than the second time, when I was exercising regularly and added specific cancer - healing nutrients and supplements to my diet. I didn't have as many side effects, felt stronger and healthier, and my recovery time was so much shorter. I was amazed at the difference it made!"*

Just as Susan was amazed at the difference good nutrition made in her health, you too can feel these same benefits by following some basic nutrition guides for your overall well-being. This includes drinking, eating and supplementation.

DRINK

"Pure Water is the World's First and Foremost Medicine. "
—*Slovakian Proverb*

Let's start with drinking, and I don't mean alcohol, soda, coffee, or juice! DRINK WATER! Why water? Your body is made up of 60% water and blood is 90% water. According to ancient Chinese healing of Thai Chi and Qi Gong, water is part of our energy source or our source of Qi. Qi, simply put, is the vital energy that guides our physical and mental processes. The brain takes in the Qi from water directly from the mouth before it goes into the stomach and intestines to be used for lubrication. The rest of the body must rely upon the digestion process to get its water. The body treats food differently than water so things like coffee, tea, or fruit juice are treated as wet food, not as water, thus depleting the brain of necessary Qi or energy. For those of you who may be skeptical of this, there is scientific evidence that caffeine, sugary drinks and alcohol cause dehydration because it takes the body even more water to remove them from your body.

Depending on the drink, it can take your body up to three times the amount of water to process those beverages. For example, it takes thirty-two ounces of water to neutralize the phosphoric and carbonic acid of one glass of soda. If you drink twelve ounces of beer, it will take your body thirty-six ounces of water to flush it out. If you don't give your body the amount of water it needs, it will take it from your bones, muscles, and most importantly, your brain. Add that to stress, and you are in certain physical distress! When you are under stress, your heart rate goes up and you breathe more heavily, therefore you lose fluid which can cause dehydration.

During times of change we are often preoccupied and stressed which causes us to forget to drink and eat well. When you're stressed, your adrenal glands produce extra cortisol– "the stress hormone"— and under chronic stress, your adrenal glands can become exhausted, resulting in lower electrolyte levels. A 2012 study published in the *British Journal of Nutrition* found that dehydration can influence mood, energy levels, and the ability to think clearly. Dehydration is the number one cause of stress in your body. In fact, it's a vicious cycle. Dehydration can cause stress, and stress can cause dehydration.

Stress can result in many of the same responses as dehydration such as increased heart rate, nausea, fatigue, and headaches. Drinking sufficient water can help reduce the negative psychological and physiological impacts of stress. By staying hydrated, you can decrease cortisol and better equip yourself to deal with everyday problems.

One of the problems with dehydration is that it mimics many of the same bodily sensations that anxiety can cause: dizziness, muscle fatigue, headache, feeling faint, increased heart rate, and nausea. These feelings can trick our minds into thinking that we are having a major medical problem, which can trigger panic for many anxiety sufferers. While staying hydrated may not get rid of anxiety entirely, it can help reduce its intensity.

Additionally, water also appears to have natural calming properties. Drinking water can be soothing, and often your body will benefit from the added hydration during times of intense stress.

How much water should you drink?

The amount of water you drink depends on your size and weight, the climate you live in and lifestyle. In general, you should try to drink between half an ounce and an ounce of water for each pound you weigh, every day. For example, if you weigh 150 pounds, that would be 75 to 150 ounces of water a day. If you're living in a hot climate and exercising a lot, you'd be on the higher end of that range; if you're in a cooler climate and mostly sedentary, you'd need less. Another quick way to check is if your urine is clear or very light yellow and has little odor, you're well-hydrated. The darker and more aromatic your urine, the more dehydrated you are.

Interesting facts about water

It lubricates the joints. Cartilage, found in joints and the disks of the spine, contains about eighty percent water. Long-term dehydration can reduce the joints' shock-absorbing ability, leading to joint pain.
It forms saliva and mucus. Saliva helps us digest our food and keeps the mouth, nose, and eyes moist. This prevents friction and damage. Drinking water also keeps the mouth clean. Consumed instead of sweetened beverages, it can also reduce tooth decay.
It delivers oxygen throughout the body. Blood is more than ninety percent water, and it carries oxygen to different parts of the body.
It boosts skin health and beauty. With dehydration, the skin can become more vulnerable to skin disorders and premature wrinkling.
It cushions the brain, spinal cord, and other sensitive tissues. Dehydration can affect brain structure and function. It is also involved in the production of hormones and neurotransmitters. Prolonged dehydration can lead to problems with thinking and reasoning.
It regulates body temperature. Water that is stored in the middle layers of the skin excrete as sweat when the body heats up. As it evaporates, it cools the body.

The digestive system depends on it. The bowel needs water to work properly. Dehydration can lead to digestive problems, constipation, and an overly acidic stomach. This increases the risk of heartburn and stomach ulcers.

It flushes body waste. Water is needed in the processes of sweating and removal of urine and feces.

It helps maintain blood pressure. A lack of water can cause blood to become thicker, increasing blood pressure.

It makes minerals and nutrients accessible. These dissolve in water, which makes it possible for them to reach different parts of the body.

It prevents kidney damage. The kidneys regulate fluid in the body. Insufficient water can lead to kidney stones and other problems.

I can attest to the last fact on this list. Moving from a cold to warm climate with increased personal stress, I would often forget to drink water, perhaps only drinking one or two glasses a day. I began having lower back pain, but being preoccupied with my divorce I ignored it, until one morning I woke up in excruciating pain, which landed me in the hospital on a morphine drip because of a kidney stone. After being pumped with fluids and spending a night in the hospital, it finally passed. My doctor told me to increase my water intake and I probably wouldn't have any more kidney stones. I followed his instructions and four years later, I've had no more problems with kidney stones. (For those of you who are wondering, kidney stones are far worse than having a baby.)

Later, when to an ER nurse, she commented that she had never seen so many people come in for kidney stones until she came to Florida. This makes sense since a large majority of the population have moved from colder parts of the country to hot climates, not realizing the need to increase water.

Just plain water is usually sufficient. While very popular, adding electrolytes to water is rarely necessary, unless you are sweating for long periods of time such as during an ultra marathon. The only time I recommend adding anything to your water is first thing in the morning. Lemon water on an empty stomach in the morning eases bloating, gas, and constipation. Lemon contains minerals that promote healthy digestion, alleviate heartburn, and stimulate healthy bowel function by reducing bloat and stimulating bowel movements. It assists the liver in cleansing the body of toxins. It reduces inflammation and eases joint pain and stiffness by preventing uric acid build up in the joints. It provides an energizing effect without the crash that often comes with caffeine. It lowers blood pressure because it is an excellent source of potassium, which can regulate blood pressure and maintain heart health – factors that reduce the risk of stroke, heart attack, anxiety, and depression. Lemon has compounds that ease breathing and calm the respiratory tract. The citric acid in lemon juice can help treat gallstones, calcium deposits, and kidney stones. It also boosts immune function, freshens breath, nourishes and soothes sore throats.

On a side note, as mentioned in the sleep section, not only is drinking water healing, but soaking in water is also healing. Simply soaking in warm water is relaxing and helps excrete water weight and toxins. I recommend bathing in Epsom salts which is pure magnesium. The magnesium draws toxins from the body, helping to improve circulation and purification.

GUIDE

Drink Water

1.Drink water first thing in the morning.
I recommend squeezing half a lemon in hot water before9 drinking or eating anything else. Consider drinking warm lemon water instead of coffee.

2.Keep track of how much water you drink during the day, drinking at least six to ten glasses of water a day depending on your body weight.

"It is chronic water shortage in the body that causes most diseases of the human body."
Dr. Fereydoon Batmanghelidj

FOOD

"Let food be thy medicine, and let medicine be thy food."
—Hippocrates

What and when to eat?

It is essential to eat nutritious food to fuel your body, especially during times of stress. There is substantial scientific evidence showing what we eat affects our body and our brain. I am convinced that the increase in depression, anxiety, panic attacks, and even ADHD has a lot to do with the toxicity in our food and environment. This includes everything from what we eat to societal expectations that did not exist in the past. Just take a look at the large amount of processed foods we consume daily containing preservatives and sugar alternatives like corn syrup, aspartame, saccharin, and stevia in comparison to fresh fruits and vegetables eaten in the past. As discussed earlier, stress greatly impacts your digestion, absorption of food and compromises your immune system.

When you're going through change, it's difficult to think about nutrition and what's happening to your body. Some of you may have no appetite and don't care to eat, depleting your body of the nutrients it needs to support the immune system, becoming more susceptible to illness, as well as losing bone and muscle mass. Some of us mindlessly stress eat, downing a whole bag of potato chips without even realizing it, putting on excess weight, causing us to be more susceptible to ailments such as high blood pressure, high cholesterol, and diabetes. The consequences of both these scenarios can result in more stress, increased anxiety, and depression. We can avoid these scenarios by eating clean, nutrient-dense food at regular intervals.

This brings us to the question of when we should eat. There are many differing views on this subject. My view is to eat balanced meals two to three times a day with a healthy snack if you so desire, having your last meal four hours before going to bed. In my experience over the past thirty-six years, having tried many eating time variations with clients, this seems to be the easiest and most successful for maintaining optimal health. Just as with sleeping at regular times, eating at regular times helps with the balance of your circadian rhythm.

Eating your meals at the same times every day with four-hour intervals will help regulate blood sugar and hormone levels. This can be effective in decreasing anxiety and depression as well as elevating your mood. Additionally, it will help your bowels be more regular, releasing harmful toxins from being stored in your body. A sign that you are healthy is having regular bowel movements at the same time every day.

Whether you are struggling with stress, anxiety, depression, or any other health issue, a balanced diet can be one method to improve overall well-being. Being aware of foods that can help us and hurt us during this time is paramount in getting through change with optimal health.

Eat REAL Food

My motto when it comes to eating is **"Variation in Moderation."** A diet rich in fruits and vegetables will supply you with almost all the vitamins and nutrients you need. Studies have compared "traditional" diets— like the Mediterranean diet and the traditional Japanese diet— to a typical "Western" diet and have shown that the risk of depression is 25% to 35% lower in those who eat a traditional diet. Scientists attribute this difference to the fact that these diets tend to be high in vegetables, fruits, unprocessed grains, fish and seafood, and contain only modest amounts of lean meats and dairy. They are also void of processed and refined foods and sugars, which are staples of the "Western" dietary pattern. In addition, many of these unprocessed foods are fermented, and therefore act as natural probiotics. Good bacteria not only influences what your gut digests and absorbs but also affects the degree of inflammation throughout your body, as well as your mood and energy level.

Eating foods of all the colors of the rainbow is a great way to get phytonutrients and antioxidants to boost your immune system and heal you. Eating foods with too much sugar, salt, preservatives, chemicals, antibiotics, and hormones can be detrimental to your immune system and hurt you. The following are some foods to consider avoiding.

Foods to Avoid

Sugar - Multiple studies have found a correlation between a diet high in refined sugars and impaired brain function and the worsening of symptoms of mood disorders such as depression. Too much sugar can cause an imbalance in the ratio of good and bad bacteria in the stomach. During high stress times, the body releases more cortisol, which helps us manage both stress and blood sugar levels. Sugary foods cause blood sugar levels to spike, causing the body to release more cortisol. Increased cortisol can cause sleep issues, headaches, unhealthy food cravings, and decreased immune response. Sugar also causes inflammation, which can be an underlying stressor causing both physical and mental symptoms. Sugars cause the pancreas to spike insulin levels, which are then followed by blood sugar crashes, causing mood swings.

Artificial sweeteners can cause headaches, metabolic and cardiovascular disease. They can cause a sugar addiction by retraining your taste buds, resulting in the desire to seek out even more sweet foods. Artificial sweeteners also have side effects that can lead to stress. Aspartame, for example, causes migraines, mood disorders, and manic episodes. In addition it blocks the production of serotonin in our brains. Aspartame is also believed to be responsible for insomnia and anxiety and has been linked to certain forms of cancer.

Salt in our diets can have a negative effect on the body's neurological system, causing fatigue and damaging the immune system. Too much sodium leads to weight gain, high blood pressure, and water retention. It can trigger panic episodes and send you down a slippery slope of anxiety, panic, and depression.

Processed foods are filled with mood-lowering or blocking ingredients. These foods usually, if not always, include refined sugar and gluten as well. They are abundant in trans-fats, artificial additives, preservatives, miscellaneous chemicals, and other synthetic ingredients. Many processed carbs, particularly standard packaged foods, are high in sodium, which causes your body to retain more fluid and forces your heart to work harder to keep the blood pumping. Processed foods contribute to bad gut health and are a major contributor to chronic anxiety as well as to many mood disorders.

Gluten filled foods contain neurotransmitters that are detrimental and exacerbate our stress. For example, wheat blocks the production of serotonin, a mood booster. Processed conventional wheat in particular is full of chemicals, pesticides and herbicides which can cause diarrhea, excess gas, abdominal bloating, joint swelling, depression, fatigue, and brain fog, all of which can make it hard to handle everyday stressors and which can be a huge trigger for anxiety symptoms. Cutting out gluten could be the difference between living with stress and anxiety versus managing it for the better.

Fried foods are difficult to digest and have very little nutrition. Combining poor food choices with unhealthy cooking processes is a surefire way to exacerbate your anxiety symptoms. Most fried foods like French fries, chicken, and onion rings are cooked in hydrogenated oil. This not only does a number on your waistline but is also terrible for your heart.

Meat (especially red meat) products are one of the most difficult to digest because they have a protein that is harder for us to breakdown. This can cause your stomach to empty more slowly, causing bloating and discomfort which can add more stress to your body.

Dairy is inflammatory and wreaks havoc on the digestive system, causing bloating, diarrhea, and constipation among other things. Evidence suggests dairy can cause chronic stress, which in turn weakens the immune system. Research also shows that people who have anxiety noticed an increase in symptoms within minutes of consuming dairy products.

Alcohol is a toxin that leads to improper mental and physical functioning by negatively impacting the levels of serotonin in the brain. Alcohol can induce the symptoms of anxiety. Alcohol also affects the nervous system and can cause hypersensitivity, increased heart rate, lowered blood sugar levels, and acute dehydration. Alcohol also lowers immune function. If you do drink, make sure you drink double amounts of water and consider moderation for quality sleep.

Caffeine is a known stimulant and has long had a reputation for triggering the body's fight-or-flight response. Caffeine can also make its users feel nervous, nauseous, lightheaded, and jittery, which are all symptoms associated with anxiety. While there are conflicting studies on the pros and cons of drinking coffee, some studies show moderate to high coffee consumption increases inflammation. In 2007, researchers from the University of Washington in Seattle found that mixing caffeine and acetaminophen can potentially cause liver damage. Consider decreasing your intake or not drinking it at all.

Foods to Eat

Just as there are foods to avoid, there are foods to eat that are especially beneficial in helping anxiety, stress, and depression. The list below is by no means extensive, and there are many more healing foods, but these are a few easy suggestions you may consider adding to your diet. The key is to think about how they will benefit you and how you can add them to your diet. This is where the mind-body connection comes into play. Imagine yourself eating healthy foods and you will do it.

Apples The saying, "An apple a day keeps the doctor away" may be truer than we thought. Apples activate our digestive, metabolic and immune systems. They have 100 percent of the phytochemicals we need to fight disease. The apple skin is the most abundant phytochemical and is a proven artery cleanser and good for colon health and bowel movements. Steamed apples can ease digestive pain.

Asparagus is high in folic acid, an essential B-vitamin that is necessary for optimal brain and nerve function. Folic acid has been proven to promote the production of neurotransmitters in the brain. Those who have reduced levels of folic acid are more prone to depression and anxiety.

Salmon is high in Omega-3 fatty acids which help ease joint pain, strengthen eye health, lower the risk of heart disease, and so much more. Omega-3 fatty acids promote optimal brain health in the prefrontal cortex, where motivation develops, and emotions are regulated. With control over motivation and emotional regulators, the brain feels less stressed out and diminishes cellular inflammation, which is one of the leading causes of anxiety and depression.

Dark, leafy greens like swiss chard, spinach, kale, arugula, and collard greens are excellent choices to add essential vitamins to the body, as they help to reduce anxiety. They are nutrient-dense and contain the highest concentration of vitamins and minerals that the body needs. They act as an armor by producing antioxidant and anti-inflammatory benefits throughout your body and brain. They are proven to reduce stress and anxiety by giving the brain blasts of folate, a critical factor in healthy neurotransmitter connections.

Fermented foods like natto, kombucha, miso, kimchi, and sauerkraut are an excellent way to return abnormal levels in the body to normal, thus improving the gut-brain connection key to reducing anxiety and depression.

Tea is almost as old as humanity itself, and it may be one of the most studied foods on the planet. Nearly every flower, herb, and weed has been used as a tea, all to varying effects. Certain kinds of tea have risen above the rest in helping to curb anxiety. Chamomile is known to calm the body and mind. According to a study completed by the University of Pennsylvania, chamomile tea significantly reduced the symptoms of anxiety when compared to placebos. Green tea is another tea that has substantial effects on anxiety. High levels of the compound L-theanine permeate the tea and relax the body.

Blueberries are a super food that battles the effects of anxiety. They have been linked to reduced feelings of depression and anxiety because of their antioxidants. They're also loaded with vitamin C, which helps lower cortisol, and therefore anxiety. A recent study found eating blueberries could help reduce the genetic and biochemical drivers behind depression and suicidal tendencies in people with post-traumatic stress disorder. Cognitive impairment has been reversed by the addition of blueberries to the diet. High doses of this fruit and other high flavonoid foods have proven to reduce the effects of Alzheimer's and other brain -impacting disorders including anxiety and depression. The brain works more efficiently when these flavonoids are readily available within the body.

Oatmeal is a healthy carbohydrate that increases serotonin production in the brain, relieving feelings of worry, nervousness, and stress. Oats are high in fiber, providing energy that lasts throughout the day and leads to an increase in resilience often found lacking in those with anxiety. Oatmeal can also help with leveling off blood sugar levels that accompany an unbalanced diet; these levels spike up and down during the day leading to an unrelaxed brain.

Nuts are known to help with anxiety and mood disorders. Brazil nuts are high in selenium, a chemical compound found in food that helps to boost one's mood by reducing inflammation within the body, which increases with anxiety. Selenium is also a powerful antioxidant that can help prevent cell damage, and it is also an anti-carcinogen, helping to prevent cancer as well. Brazil nuts and almonds are also a great source of vitamin E, another mighty antioxidant, which can be significantly beneficial for treating anxiety, as some studies have shown that low levels of vitamin E can lead to depression in some people. Anti-inflammatory omega-3 fatty acids in the form of alpha-linolenic acid (ALA), are found in walnuts and pecans, which can help reduce symptoms of anxiety and depression.

Eggs contain high-quality protein including critical amino acids that produce the vital neurotransmitters dopamine and serotonin,

117

which improve one's overall mental health. Egg yolks, in particular, are an excellent source of vitamin D, a known vitamin that promotes healthy brain function and can help reduce symptoms of anxiety and depression. They also contain tryptophan, an amino acid that helps the body create serotonin, a chemical neurotransmitter that helps regulate mood, behavior, memory, and sleep. Serotonin is also believed to improve brain function and relieve anxiety. I recommend farm-fresh, pasture-raised eggs, versus commercial eggs raised in chicken factories, fed antibiotics, and subjected to high levels of stress. They are richer in nutrients, which can help combat elevated cortisol levels and inflammation.

Dark chocolate acts as a natural antidepressant, making us feel better because it contains tyrosine, which is linked to an increase of dopamine. Cocoa in dark chocolate is known to facilitate the release of serotonin by relaxing the blood vessels in the brain. It also releases endorphins which allow us to feel happy and can also reduce cortisol levels to alleviate feelings of stress or anxiety. It is a rich source of polyphenols, especially flavonoids. Flavonoids help reduce neuroinflammation, improve blood circulation throughout the body, boosting blood flow to the brain and promoting its ability to adapt to stressful environments. It also contains a high tryptophan level, which the body converts into mood-enhancing neurotransmitters, as well as magnesium, which may help to reduce the symptoms of depression. Be sure to eat this in moderation, as it is high in calories and contains added sugars and fats.

Chia seeds are loaded with essential nutrients including iron, calcium, and magnesium. They are also a great source of the good fats Omega-3. Just a handful of chia seeds added to your daily diet can aid digestion, protect your heart and boost immunity. Researchers have found that Omega-3 fats can help in fighting depression and mood swings.

Kiwi has potent antioxidant properties, which help boost immune system function and enhance cell protection and repair. They are full of nutrients like vitamin C, vitamin K, vitamin E, folate, and potassium and are a good source of fiber. Research suggests that eating kiwifruit may have significant benefits for sleep. Kiwi seeds contain fiber and a mood-boosting nutrient called alpha-linolenic acid. ALA is a plant-based omega-3 fatty acid that helps to control an inflammatory compound linked to depression.

Sunflower seeds are rich in the B complex vitamins, which are essential for a healthy nervous system, and are a good source of phosphorus, magnesium, iron, calcium, potassium, protein and vitamin E. They also contain trace minerals, zinc, manganese, copper, chromium and carotene as well as monounsaturated and polyunsaturated fatty acids- types of 'good' fat that may help to protect the arteries. Sunflower seeds are a natural source of zinc and are immune boosters. They may also help protect against heart disease, while their vitamin B can help in the fight against stress.

Honey is rich in minerals such as iron, calcium, and magnesium. The glucose in honey is absorbed by the body quickly, giving an immediate energy boost, while the fructose provides sustained energy since it is absorbed more slowly. Honey has also been found to keep levels of blood sugar fairly constant in comparison to other types of sugar. Honey also releases serotonin, a neurotransmitter that improves your mood, and the body converts serotonin into melatonin, a chemical compound that regulates the length and quality of sleep. Honey's antioxidant and antibacterial properties help improve the digestive system and **boost immunity**. It is also a powerhouse of **antioxidants**, which are very effective for the removal of free radicals from the body. Drink a teaspoon of honey daily, along with your morning lemon water.

Vitamin D and B Vitamins and Folic acid

A study published in the Journal of Affective Disorders believes there is sufficient evidence proving that vitamin D helps with depression. The problem is that most people are trying to get Vitamin D from supplements, and it is not absorbing into their body. The best way to get Vitamin D is through sunshine. Just ten to twenty minutes a day can do wonders for your mood. Similar to vitamin D, researchers have found that a deficiency in B vitamins, such as B12 and folic acid, can trigger depression in some individuals. I suggest getting these through food. You can get folic acid and B12 through a variety of foods to include legumes, asparagus, eggs, leafy greens, beets, citrus fruits, Brussel sprouts, broccoli, papaya, avocado, nuts and seeds, nori, shiitake mushrooms, and wild caught fish and seafood.

According to Susan Taylor Mayne, a professor at the Yale School of Public Health's Division of Chronic Disease Epidemiology, "The best way to get vitamins is through food, not vitamin pills. A major problem with supplements is that they deliver vitamins out of context, she says. The vitamins found in fruit, vegetables and other foods come with thousands of other phytochemicals, or plant nutrients that are not essential for life but may protect against cancer, cardiovascular disease, Alzheimer's disease and other chronic ailments."

With the exception of pregnant women, who should consider taking folic acid supplements and people over fifty years of age, since absorption of vitamins in the digestive tract becomes less efficient with age, I highly recommend trying to improve your diet before taking supplements. Food tastes better than a pill, is often less expensive, and the fiber content helps to have regular bowel movements to eliminate toxins. Pills just can't compare.

Herbal Supplements

Alternative and holistic medicine practitioners use herbs and many other remedies to assist people with health and overall well-being. I am a huge proponent of using these. With that being said, if you are taking medications to treat anxiety, always do your own research and talk to your doctor before trying an herbal supplement or remedy. Below are a few herbs you may want to try.

Ginger is a powerhouse with over 100 compounds and fifty antioxidants. It is most commonly used as a digestive aid and anti-inflammatory, but it also has mood boosting properties. Ginger increases blood flow to the brain and modulates blood sugar levels, keeping energy levels up during the day. It also increases the level of two of the most important brain chemicals, serotonin and dopamine. It is said that ginger tea can elevate mood and banish negative feelings and that even a whiff of ginger can lift your spirits.

Curcumin is a powerful herb with over 100 anti-inflammatory, antioxidant, antiviral, antibacterial, and antifungal. It also acts as an antidepressant. Curcumin increases production of dopamine and enhances noradrenaline and tryptophan levels. Numerous studies show its ability to improve levels of neurotransmitters and thereby improve mood. One study found that when combined with some antidepressants it improves their effectiveness. Another study found that it was as effective as Prozac without the side effects.

Elderberry is packed with antioxidants and vitamins that may boost your immune system. The phytochemicals in elderberry have been linked to an improved mood. Furthermore, it has

been shown to relieve some symptoms of mental/emotional disorders such as anxiety and depression.
.

Ashwagandha has long been recommended for its supposedly refreshing and energizing effects in Ayurveda (the traditional medicine of India). Studies have shown that Ashwagandha has stress-fighting effects. One study found that Ashwagandha root extract effectively increased resistance to stress and improved quality of life.

Ginseng, specifically Panax ginseng (also known as Korean, Asian, or Chinese ginseng), is often praised for its anti-stress properties. Research suggests that ginseng may help stabilize the nervous system response and improve cognition for people who are exposed to high levels of stress. There is also some research reporting anti-depressant-like ingredients.

Chamomile is used most often for upset stomach, but it has also been found to help calm nerves and improve sleep. In a study published by the BMC Complementary and Alternative Medicine, chamomile was also found to improve daytime functioning in people with insomnia.

Licorice is another popular option that may have stress-relieving benefits. While more research is needed, there is some evidence that licorice tea may have some benefits for promoting stress relief and reducing feelings of anxiety. A 2011 study found that there were some reductions in stress from licorice tea.

Peppermint is one of the best allies when it comes to relieving stress and anxiety. The menthol present in the herb is known to be a muscle relaxant and is antispasmodic in nature, helping you relax amidst ongoing mental stress.

Essential Oils

Copaiba oil has a plethora of benefits when taken internally. The main constituent of Copaiba oil is Beta-caryophyllene, which helps soothe anxious feelings. In addition to its emotional benefits, Beta-caryophyllene promotes healthy nervous, cardiovascular, and immune system function. The oil also contains powerful antioxidants that boost immune health. Copaiba oil is a well-loved oil because it relieves discomfort and promotes overall health.

Lavender is high in linalool and when taken internally reduces anxious feelings. Its calming aroma can also help cut through feelings of stress and promote relaxation. Studies suggest that it may be useful for treating anxiety, insomnia, depression, and restlessness. Researchers monitored sleep cycles with brain scans and found that lavender increased slow-wave sleep, instrumental for slowing heartbeat and relaxing muscles. Subjects slept more soundly on a lavender night.

Peppermint provides relief from stress, depression, and mental exhaustion due to its refreshing nature. It is also effective against feeling anxious and restless. Peppermint oil powerfully affects and improves mental clarity and raises energy levels. Apply to the back of the neck and shoulders repeatedly to keep energy levels up during the day. Inhale before and during a workout to help boost your mood and reduce fatigue. Diffuse peppermint oil in the room to improve concentration and accuracy. Rub a drop of oil under your nose to help improve concentration and alertness. If you're trying to cut back on caffeine, this may be a blessing to combat your mid-afternoon lull.

Geranium is known to reduce feelings of stress, anxiety, sadness, fatigue, and tension. It enhances a general sense of well-being and relaxation while offering relief to those suffering from insomnia. It has a sweet, floral fragrance that calms and relaxes the body and mind. It is considered to have a gently- relaxing effect on the mood and works as a natural antidepressant. For stress relief, the combination of peppermint, lavender, and geranium essential oils added to a warm bath helps relieve stiffness while absorbed through the skin.

GUIDE

Keep a Food Journal

1. Take a moment and imagine yourself eating healthy foods that can heal and help you through this time of change.

2. Write down a list of healthy foods you can see yourself eating this week. On your next grocery trip, buy those foods and incorporate them into your diet.

---

3. Write in your food journal and include what time you eat each day and what foods you eat. Note how you feel on the bottom of each page. Pay attention to how eating different foods makes you feel, not just in the moment, but the next day. Food can affect us a day or even two days after we eat. This will help you recognize what foods affect your physical body as well as your mood.

CHAPTER 13
EXERCISE

"Exercise not only changes your body, it changes your mind, attitude and mood."

Your body was meant to move! Just take a look at your elbows and knees and notice how they automatically move in your daily activities. When going through difficult changes in our lives, often we can barely get out of bed, let alone want to move. We may become depressed and neglect self-care.

Exercise is one of the first things that seem to go, when it should be the first thing we do to get us through the day. Exercise reduces levels of the body's stress hormones, such as adrenaline and cortisol. It also stimulates the production of endorphins, chemicals in the brain that are the body's natural painkillers and mood elevators.

Several studies found that heart-pumping, endorphin-boosting workouts decrease depression and promote happiness. Research suggests that just thirty minutes a day of exercise can boost your mood in addition to making your body healthier. This doesn't have to be a grandiose workout. In fact, virtually any form of exercise or movement can decrease your stress and increase your fitness level. The most important thing is to pick an activity that you enjoy. Maryanne's experience is a great example of what can happen when we do this.

Maryanne wanted to lose twenty pounds. Even though she walked on her treadmill every morning, she wasn't having much success. After changing her diet and adding some resistance training, she still wasn't getting the results she wanted. We talked about what other physical activity she might like to do. She expressed that she had always wanted to try ballroom dancing and decided to add that two times per week, and within three months lost twenty pounds. Since she was a daycare provider during the day and didn't get the chance to do much for herself, this provided her with the added benefit of getting out a couple of nights a week doing something she enjoyed, which helped her relieve stress as well as maintain a healthy weight.

Exercise is also a potent remedy for anxiety, and just five minutes of exercise can trigger anti-anxiety responses in the body. Research indicates that regular exercise that is part of a consistent routine can help boost both sleep duration and sleep quality. Being physically active requires you to expend energy and, therefore, helps you feel more tired and ready to rest at the end of the day. Additionally, scientific evidence indicates that exercise can be an effective natural therapy for insomnia. Aerobic exercise may be particularly effective in helping to reduce insomnia symptoms.

Research has found that the benefits of exercise for insomnia are not immediate but kick in over time. Studies have also found that exercise can help lower the severity of sleep- disordered breathing and may help to reduce the severity of obstructive sleep apnea. Understanding how crucial sleep is to your health, exercise should be a **"must do"** and not just a "maybe" in your daily routine.

When is the best time to exercise?

The best time to exercise is when it feels best for you! It depends on your bio time and what you want to achieve. Morning people like to get up early and start the day moving. Night people prefer to work out in the evening. Some like to split up their day and prefer an afternoon workout at lunch or around 3:00 or 4:00pm. There really is no right or wrong time to exercise. Various studies show benefits for exercising at different times of day which are listed below, but in reality, it ultimately does depend on you and what works for you.

For example, one of my clients had to walk before 7:00pm, or she had trouble sleeping. My son, on the other hand, works out at 10:00pm and sleeps great.

- Morning exercise gives a particular boost to deep sleep.
- Physical performance peaks later in the day.
- A late-in-the-day workout can help suppress your appetite and make it easier to avoid overeating in the evening.
- Exercising before eating breakfast can help you burn more fat during the day.
- Muscle strength reaches optimal levels in the late afternoon and early evening for most bio types.

Before beginning a long workout exercise session, I suggest incorporating visualization and breath work. Starting a workout with a short meditation to focus on the body works wonders! End with a short stretch and resting segment focusing on relaxing the nerve endings and connecting the body to the mind to recognize the benefits of the physical workout. Scheduling your workouts on your calendar and being consistent is key to success.

GUIDE

Schedule daily exercise in your calendar.

For the next week, spend each day getting your body moving with at least thirty minutes of exercise. Set aside a location and time. Then go for a walk, hit the treadmill at the gym, or turn on your favorite music and dance around your room. This isn't supposed to be a marathon-level of activity; it's just to get your body moving a bit more than usual. Notice how much better you feel after getting in some exercise.

Can't find thirty minutes? Add just five to ten minutes of short heart-pumping exercise like jumping jacks, burpees, jump rope, or even walking up and down your stairs ten times. Can't jump or go upstairs– check out my YouTube videos or Facebook page at mylifechangesolutions.com for modified short workouts).

PART V
HAPPINESS

CHAPTER 14
WHAT IS HAPPINESS?

"Happiness is the highest desire and ambition of all human beings." —*Aristotle*

Happiness is something we all seek no matter what our circumstances. You may know people who always seem to be happy regardless of what happens to them or what challenges they have, yet others always seem to be unhappy, even when life is good. What makes one person happy and another not? By definition happiness is a state of being and seems to be different for everyone. What is happiness to you? Here are a few responses from a short survey asking that question.

"Happiness is that feeling that comes over you when you know life is good, and you can't help but smile."

"Happiness is accepting that life is full of suffering and being okay with it all."

"Happiness is when you love someone more than yourself."

"Happiness is when all the puzzle pieces of my life fit in all the right places."

My personal definition of happiness is being content and finding joy in living my best life. If we all see happiness somewhat differently, are there specific things that bring everyone happiness? Philosophers, psychologists, and scientists have spent a lifetime trying to figure that out. There are over 30,000 books written on the subject. There is a longitudinal study done over eighty years by Harvard University to determine what brings long-term happiness, and that research revealed that there are some very specific factors that bring us happiness.

Groundbreaking research in positive psychology has shown that the behaviors and habits we engage in, from gratitude to kindness to mindfulness, can lead to an enduring happiness. Thanks to some of that research we have an understanding of what we can do to give ourselves the best chance of being happy. The following are some interesting findings about happiness.

1. You control about half your happiness level. Although the exact level will vary from individual to individual, it appears that up to about fifty percent of our happiness levels are preset by genetics or our environment. That means that about fifty percent of our happiness is within our power to raise or lower.

2. Money doesn't buy happiness. Once we get to a certain level of income that is enough to pay our bills and keep us in the lifestyle we've grown accustomed to, more money doesn't result in more happiness. One exception to this is that people who give money away appear to sustain greater levels of happiness over time than those who don't.

3. Lottery winnings create only temporary, short-term happiness. Winning the lottery makes people happy in the moment, but that happiness fades fairly quickly, and then people return to their prior level of happiness. In the long run, people who won the lottery appear to be no happier than those who haven't.

4. Relationships are a key factor in long-term happiness. While research has demonstrated that this effect is strongest for married people, other research has shown that strong social connections with others are important to our happiness. The more of these you have, generally, the happier you will be.

5. Focus on experiences, not stuff. People who spend their time and money on doing things together, whether it be taking a vacation or going on a day outing, report higher levels of happiness than those who buy a bigger house, a more expensive car, or more stuff. Buying stuff only buys artificial, temporary happiness. Our memories keep an emotional photograph of experiences, whereas material things don't make as big an emotional imprint in our brains.

As you can see, circumstances, possessions, experiences, and people in our lives all have an impact on our happiness, but it is the actual chemical reactions that happen in our brain that affect our mood. There are four main neurochemicals, hormones, and neurotransmitters that are generated in the brain and are fundamentally responsible for creating the sensations and emotions that make us happy.

During times of change these hormones can get out of balance decreasing our happiness. I have made mention of some of these throughout this book, but a description of each will give you a better understanding of the role each plays in connection with happiness. It may also help us understand why taking medication isn't always effective, as our happiness relies on a delicate balance of our hormones. A recent medical journal states that medication may help raise some hormone levels, thus making life more manageable, but may not increase one's level of happiness. The good news is that the more you take care of yourself, the better the balance will be, and the happier you will feel.

There are four main hormones that affect our mood and what we can do naturally to increase our level of happiness.

Dopamine is known as the "feel-good" hormone. It's a neurotransmitter that's an important part of your brain's reward system. Dopamine is a striving emotion, responsible for reward-driven behavior and pleasure seeking. Every type of reward-seeking behavior that has been studied increases the level of dopamine transmission in the brain. When you score a goal or accomplish a task, you receive a pleasurable hit of dopamine in your brain, which tells you you've done a good job. You can also get a natural dose of dopamine when you perform acts of kindness toward others. Some research has found that it only takes thoughts of loving kindness to bring on the dopamine high. Studies also show that music is linked with our deepest reward systems and raises our levels of dopamine.

Oxytocin is often called the "love hormone" because it is primarily associated with loving touch and close relationships. Oxytocin is a peptide hormone composed of nine amino acids released from the pituitary gland. It is essential for childbirth, breastfeeding, and strong parent-child bonding. This hormone can also help promote trust, empathy, and bonding in relationships. Oxytocin levels generally increase with physical affection like kissing, cuddling, sex, and even petting an animal. When released it makes us feel empathy, which helps us feel close and bonded to others. It facilitates social interaction and is associated with positive social behavior.

Serotonin might be considered the "confidence hormone." It allows people to put themselves in situations that will boost self-esteem, increase feelings of worthiness, and create a sense of belonging. It is a hormone and neurotransmitter that helps regulate your mood as well as your sleep, appetite, digestion, learning ability, and memory. Eighty percent of serotonin exists in the gut. Exercise and happy thoughts also stimulate production of this chemical. You can increase serotonin by accomplishing activities like volunteering. This will reinforce your sense of self-worth, purpose, and belonging. Studies have shown that any exercise – from riding a bike or running to getting sun or a massage l will increase serotonin. Another way to up your serotonin is by reflecting on what you have in your life. For example, experiences, people, and things that make you feel grateful, loved, and important will affect your serotonin levels. Your brain will produce serotonin regardless of whether a situation is imagined or is recalled. Some ways to do this are through positive affirmations, reflecting, writing a gratitude journal, or looking through old pictures of good times.

Endorphins are opioid neuropeptides, which means they are produced by the central nervous system to help us deal with physical pain. They also make us feel lightheaded and even giddy at times. One way to induce endorphins is through exercise. One study found that as little as thirty minutes of walking on a treadmill for ten days in a row was sufficient to produce a significant reduction in depression among clinically- depressed subjects. Endorphins are responsible for masking pain or discomfort, which explains their association with the "fight or flight" response. When it comes to designing happiness, endorphins help you power through. You will see in Erica's experience with running that endorphins are what allow her to push farther and harder as she works towards distant goals.

Erica's story

Life certainly did not turn out as Erica had expected. After the loss of her husband, she found herself alone raising six children and pregnant. Even though life did not turn out at all how she had hoped, she was able to work through change while finding joy and purpose. As a child she was taught to be goal oriented, meticulous and thoughtful, and she always accomplished the goals she set for herself. Her husband's cancer was the first time she realized she could not control what happened. She recognized that while she couldn't control the situation, she could control how she responded.

This took a lot of self-reflection, visualizing, and making lists of things she could control and ways in which she could respond. She told herself that even in the most difficult situations, in those dark, dark moments, the one thing she could choose to do was find *one good thing* every day.

She connected with a community of widowed friends online and found that connecting with people who had similar situations was extremely helpful. She had always felt a purpose in motherhood but being so invested in taking care of her husband and children, she felt she had lost herself.

After she got into the swing of things, she recognized that she needed something to look forward to, so she started exercising, reading, and going out socially with girlfriends. She sensed she needed to connect with others. At thirty years old, she had a feeling she would get remarried. Two and a half years after her husband passed, she met Spencer on the online widow support group. They were just friends supporting each other for quite some time before their relationship became romantic.

When they got married, they had some huge obstacles, not the least of which was eleven children. She recognized that her experiences growing up had taught her she could accomplish whatever she put her mind to. She found naming the obstacle and having something specific to work towards helped.

She realized that with eleven kids, she and Spencer needed to make time to spend with each other. They decided to get up early while the kids were asleep and exercise together, kind of like a daily mini-date. Spencer loved to run, so Erica took up running. This was difficult for her but also rewarding. She said, "At first running a mile was terrible! I did it. Then I did two. The sense of accomplishment is one of the most awarding things in my life. It gives me a high level of happiness!"

Like Erica, we may experience challenges that bring us some amount of sadness. Without those, we would not know what happiness is. Still, we can get through those challenging times and find happiness along the way. Erica naturally did many essential things to help her find happiness during difficult changes in her life. Studies confirm that we are able to create a greater appreciation for feelings of happiness after negative experiences. The research found that it is possible to increase the hormones in our brain naturally by incorporating these evidence-based happiness practices.

The following seven guides can help you find greater happiness. Some may be easy for you, while others may be more challenging. The challenge itself can bring you more happiness! Working towards a goal and achieving it are significant ways in which to bring about happiness.

SEVEN GUIDES TO HAPPINESS

1. BE GRATEFUL
2. HELP OTHERS
3. PRACTICE FORGIVENESS
4. HAVE A PURPOSE
5. TAKE TIME FOR SELF CARE
6. DEVELOP QUALITY RELATIONSHIPS
7. LOOK FORWARD TO SOMETHING

CHAPTER 15
BE GRATEFUL

"Expect Nothing, Appreciate Everything"

"Happiness will never come to those who fail to appreciate what they already have." —Buddha

When we express gratitude, our brain releases dopamine and serotonin, two crucial neurotransmitters responsible for elevating our emotions. They enhance our mood immediately, making us feel happy from the inside. Numerous studies have found that just being grateful can increase our happiness by up to 25 percent. Gratitude is a positive emotional state in which we recognize and appreciate what we have in life. Researchers have found that gratitude and happiness are always strongly correlated and taking time to experience gratitude will not only make us happier but healthier as well. Gratitude helps us experience more positive emotions, enjoy good experiences, face adversity, and develop and maintain relationships of strength. When we find gratitude in just being alive and living in the moment, the past and the future no longer seem as important. We value each new day as a gift to enjoy.

During the COVID quarantine, some people felt lonely, isolated, and distraught. Some were convinced this was the worst disaster the world had ever seen, while others were grateful for the opportunity to take a break from the world. Those who were distraught and unhappy could only think about what they were missing like going to restaurants, shopping, movies, or about the economic impact. Meanwhile, those who were grateful were happy to have a safe place to live and enjoyed spending more time with family, either in person or virtually.

It can be challenging to be grateful when we go through difficult times, especially when life hasn't turned out as expected. Unmet expectations have a huge effect on our inability to be happy and find gratitude. We have certain expectations in life. For example, when we get married, we expect to grow old together; when we have children, we expect to see them live to adulthood; when we get a job we expect to enjoy it and keep it; and we expect our health to be good with no life-altering illnesses.

Our expectations of what we think our life should be can make it difficult for us to be grateful and find happiness. One day when feeling sad about my unmet expectations of having a united family I found a sign while shopping, that said, **"Expect Nothing, Appreciate Everything."** At that moment, I realized that while my life is not as I expected, I have so much to be grateful for. This brought me such a good feeling that I purchased the sign and now display it in my home to remind me how just being grateful in the moment and not expecting anything brings happiness to my soul.

When we are grateful, it is much easier to reframe or see things in a different perspective. Daily gratitude meditation, prayer or keeping a gratitude journal are ways to improve mood and increase happiness. It's hard to be unhappy when we think of all we are grateful for. You may want to try it right now. Think of something you are grateful for and notice how you feel in the very moment that you have the grateful thought. You will probably notice that while you had the grateful thought, you felt happier. We cannot have two thoughts at the same time, so it is impossible to think a positive and negative thought at the same time.

As discussed in chapter one, how we think makes all the difference. Our thoughts can hold us back from happiness, or they can bring us happiness. If we habitually see the negative and are unable to see past our expectations, we will find it difficult to be happy. If on the other hand, we can let go of our expectations and turn our thoughts to gratitude, we can move forward and find joy no matter what our circumstances. An example of this is Chris's story.

Chris's Story

At thirty-five, Chris was diagnosed with systematic Lupus. He owned a successful business and enjoyed helping others as he served in a leadership position in his church. He took great care of his body by eating healthy and exercising.

When I interviewed Chris, his first words to me were, *"I feel like I'm the luckiest person alive."* I was surprised by this statement, because at the time he was going through his third bout of cancer. Just a few weeks prior he had learned that his cancer had returned, and doctors told him he could die within a couple of months. The last time he had cancer, he was laid up for a year with a hip replacement surgery that had gotten infected. After that he was on crutches and used a cane for another year. On top of all that, he had a stroke. So, this time when he heard the cancer had returned, he felt really low for a few days. He then came to the realization that his life might be shorter than some, but longer than others. He remembered praying, *"If that's what my fate is, I'll accept it, but I'd like to stay and see my future grandkids."*

Chris decided he had to move forward with faith. He spoke with admiration and respect about his family and shared how grateful he was for them. He said, *"My wife is an all-star, and has truly been a foundation for our family, especially when I was gone with work so much of the time."* He shared how grateful he is that his kids are all active in their faith, moving forward at exciting times of their lives, graduating from college, and getting married.

He told me how difficult it was to lose both his father and sister, but how grateful he was for the close relationship he had with both of them. Watching his dad die of cancer was difficult, but because of his faith he felt confident he would see him again. Three years prior his older sister was in a freak zip-lining accident and died tragically. Chris said, *"The horror was overwhelming. It was a horrible, horrible experience. Even though I think she was gone before her time I had to accept what happened. She was beautiful person full of love, kindness and wisdom."* Chris's ability to be grateful for the good relationship he had with both his father and sister seemed to be fundamental in his ability to find joy amongst his sadness.

When I asked him how he remains in such good spirits, he said, *"I believe that God shapes us how we need to be. At the time I was at my lowest, a thought came to me: Do I not only have faith to be healed, but do I have faith not to be healed? At that moment I couldn't say yes, but now I can."*

Chris's desire to live life to the fullest is still strong, He said, *"I have a fighting chance, and I'm in otherwise good health. My goal is to get well, go to my kid's golf tournaments, and travel all over the world with my wife. I feel confident we will. I'll get better, and we'll have these opportunities."*

Not only was Chris able to find gratitude, but he also practiced many of the essential things that bring happiness like hope, self-care, helping others, and having things to look forward to.

As we learn to be more grateful in our lives, we can feel as Chris does: We too, are the "luckiest people alive", no matter what our circumstances.

One of the biggest reasons for feeling unhappy or sad is that we don't count our blessings. Instead, we focus on what we lack. Most of the time we are not aware we compare ourselves to others, like when we are on social media, watching T.V. or hanging out with friends. Once we are aware, we can start thinking about all the things we DO have, the things we love, the people we have, and all of the blessings that life has given us.

GUIDE
Keep a Gratitude Journal

1. Take a few minutes every morning and night to meditate or pray about three things you are grateful for. They can be little things or big things (for example, *"I'm thankful to be alive,"* *"I'm thankful for a sunny day," "I'm thankful I'm not in pain," "I'm thankful my children are healthy"*). Take a moment to write them down in a word or short phrase.

_____

_____

_____

_____

_____

_____

2. At the end of the day, think about things that you were thankful for that day (good day at work, kids didn't fight, a friend called). Share them with a partner or friend or write them down.

_____

_____

_____

_____

_____

"Most people are about as happy as they make up their minds to be."—Abraham Lincoln

CHAPTER 16
HELP OTHERS

"Helping one person may not change the whole world, but it may change the world for one person."

It may seem counterintuitive to help others when you are going through change and are overwhelmed, stressed, or down, but research shows that it can lift your spirit and increase dopamine in your brain. The research found that even just thinking about ways in which we can help others can increase levels of dopamine. Helping others not only promotes good feelings, but also distracts us from our own problems at the same time. One woman continued to serve the women in her church even while going through a divorce and found that by helping others, her problems didn't seem quite as bad. One man would always find ways to help his neighbor, a single mother. When she asked why he was always so helpful, he replied, *"I was raised by a single mom and know how hard it was for her, so it makes me feel good when I can help you with things you can't do."*

Finding things that contribute to others and the world brings us happiness. Research shows that happy people are motivated to do kind things for others. When you feel overwhelmed by your circumstance, finding someone else to help may be just the thing to lift your spirits. These do not have to be over-the-top or time-intensive acts, but they should be things that help or impact another person.

147

How does one get through the sadness of an extreme loss of a child? Having dealt closely with one of the families who were affected by the Parkland, Florida school shooting, I had the experience of seeing how they were able to cope with the sadness and move forward. This family was understandably distraught and saddened to have their daughter taken from them so suddenly. Getting up every day and living their best lives is difficult. There is not a day that goes by that they do not miss their daughter, but instead of dwelling on their pain, they choose to focus on their good memories of her kindness. They celebrate and honor her with their nonprofit Kindness Foundation in her name, and every year on her birthday month they have a twenty-two-day Kindness Challenge.

You may be asking, *"How can this help me lose weight, change my health, or make other changes in my life?"* When we do kind things for others, our self-esteem increases, which can motivate us to make changes in our own lives. When we are helping others, we are not focusing on food or how bad we feel. Remember, it is impossible to think two thoughts at the same time! When we help others, dopamine increases and notably reduces depression and lessens stress.

GUIDE

Help Others

Do at least one act of service every day.
Find ways to help others, neighbors, church, shelters, pet rescues, etc. For example, help your colleague with something, give a few dollars or some time to a cause you believe in, say something kind to a stranger, write a thank you note, give blood, call a family member or friend. At the end of each day, make a note, either mentally or in your journal, of what you did. (Don't know what to do? Meditate or pray to be inspired to know what you can do or who might need your help).

CHAPTER 17
FORGIVENESS

"Holding on to anger is like grasping a hot coal with the intent of throwing it at someone else; you are the one getting burned. " —Buddha

How do you just let go and forgive someone who has wronged you? How do you let the pain wash away? Forgiveness is a conscious, deliberate decision to release feelings of resentment or vengeance toward a person or group who has harmed you, regardless of whether they actually deserve your forgiveness.

Since our natural instinct is to protect ourselves, we will do everything we can to prevent pain. When someone hurts us, we naturally want to hold onto that memory so we won't forget it, so it doesn't happen to us again. How do we go against the force of our natural instincts? We have to train our brain to recognize that forgiving is far more beneficial for us than not forgiving. Resentment brings us suffering.

Forgiveness brings happiness! Part of going through life means sometimes experiencing hurt, betrayal, injury, and loss. Few of us fully realize the huge impact the ability to forgive can have on our happiness. When we can't forgive, we often ruminate about how we've been wronged and sometimes even plot revenge. Researchers find unforgiving people tend to be hateful, angry, and hostile, therefore causing them anxiety, depression, and often neurotic behaviors. Preoccupation with a transgression or hostility towards another can actually make us physically sick. As the saying goes, *"Resentment is like taking a poison and waiting for the other person to die."*

Although forgiveness is one of the hardest things to do, it is also one of the most freeing. Think about how much time you waste on a daily basis loathing a certain person who has wronged you. When you let the person who has done you wrong continue to be in your thoughts you let them walk away with your happiness. Forgiveness doesn't mean we will forget the past or condone bad behavior, nor does it mean everything will go back to normal and we'll have to act as if the incident never happened. It means we are willing to let go of our feeling of resentment. Forgiveness is not something that we do for someone else's sake; it is for our own inner peace. It is truly a gift we give to ourselves!

By releasing all the negative obsessive thoughts surrounding the person or situation bringing you pain, you can open your mind to positive, happier thoughts. Forgiveness clears negative energy from our bodies and opens up pathways for positive energy to flow creating balance in our life and space in our head and heart for new and exciting opportunities and, most importantly, happiness. If you are skeptical of this, Scott's story may inspire you.

Scott's Story

After getting his undergraduate degree, Scott was counting on getting accepted to his Alma Mater for his master's degree. When that didn't happen, he had to wait a year to get into another graduate school. Instead of being resentful, he took the opportunity to work where he had previously interned for a year. Scott was encouraged to become an administrator and sent to an eight-month program to get his administrators license. Twelve years later, after being an administrator, he realized he had a passion for what he was doing and started his own business. He owned the business for five years before

152

selling it to build another business with a couple of partners. They were very successful and he felt great about all they accomplished, until he found out that his partners stole millions of dollars and brought down the business. He lost almost everything. He had never held grudges before then, but this knocked him down professionally. At first, he was bitter. The partners never paid him back and never said sorry. He had to learn to forgive them.

At this time, he was also a leader in his church and found himself having to teach about forgiveness, but he struggled with this as his mind dealt with thoughts like, *"I did no wrong; I don't feel like I need to forgive ; they stole from me."* He went on to say, *"It came down to the point that I just realized, I teach the principle of forgiveness. I need to practice it."* He counseled with other church leaders, who never told him what to do but guided him and led him. He pondered, read scriptures, and listened to spiritual talks on his drive to work. The process of working through it finally brought him to the realization that he had to forgive. He said, *"I had this big spot in my personal life, and I couldn't get across the finish line. I realized I had to leave that money on the table. I could not get it back. I tried. I accepted that the money was gone and I would never see it."*

As soon as he felt he could honestly forgive, doors opened up for him, and he started a bigger, better company. Scott insightfully explained, *"We were instrumental in helping so many more people. That never would have happened had I not lost the other business.," When bad things happen, we often narrow our vision and look for the bad. I felt so much better once I forgave."* One day, much later, he received a call from one of the partners who was considering ending his life. Scott talked him out of the situation. Scott realized this man had no one else to turn to. At that point he knew he had forgiven him. He commented, *"He still calls me from time to time. I'll talk*

*to him. I won't go into business with him again. But I'll be
kind and friendly."*

Scott's last statement is important. While forgiveness is essential to our happiness, it does not mean we forget or condone
another's behavior. At times it may seem impossible to do this,
but as we saw with Scott, it is possible. Forgiveness is a learnable
skill that anybody can master if we are willing to train our brain
and let go of our pain. By holding onto our pain, we may think
that we are empowering ourselves, but instead we are just increasing our suffering. Holding onto past hurt leaves a canker on
our soul, making it impossible to let go of the past. When we live
in the past, we can't move forward.

It's important to feel our emotions, but we need to know when
to let go and write a new chapter in the story of our life. It is a
commitment to ourself that we will no longer let an experience
negatively impact our life, and that we are ready to choose happiness over bitterness, resentment, and despair.

As Scott expressed, it may take time to work through, but it is
the ultimate form of healing.

I wish I could give you a magic pill to help you through the
process of forgiveness, but we all have different ways to get
there. What I can do is give you some ideas that have helped others and encourage you to be committed to the process of forgiveness. Once you have committed, you may find the inspiration
you need that will work for you. When we forgive, it increases
our self-esteem, hope, health, and happiness!

The following guide is a forgiveness meditation that has
helped many of my clients and groups. Some have experienced
immediate peace. Others have found it takes patience and practice.

GUIDE
Forgiveness Meditation

Step 1. Sit comfortably with your eyes closed. Breathe in through your nose and out through your mouth allowing your body to feel relaxed. Breathing slowly and deeply, feel yourself present, relaxing with each breath. Allow an image to come of Someone for whom you have anger or resentment. Let yourself see that person now as if he/she were sitting across from you in a chair. Look at that person and say, *"I forgive you."* Soften toward that person. Imagine her coming into your heart just for now. Breathe in. Hold her there in your heart for a moment, breathing in and breathing out, staying present with her, relaxing, feeling forgiveness for her, breathing in and out. Allow yourself to be there for a minute or two more and then let her go, saying, *"I forgive you."* Be aware of yourself again, breathing in through your nose and out through your mouth, breathing slowly and deeply, feeling yourself present, here and now, relaxing with each breath.

Step 2. Visualize someone you have harmed in some way. Visualize him as if he were sitting in a chair across from you. Look at that person and say to him, *"Forgive me, for whatever I may have done to harm you, intentionally or unintentionally. Forgive me."* Open your heart to this person and imagine him opening his heart to you. Hold him in your mind and your heart for a few moments, breathing in and out, staying soft, relaxing, feeling forgiveness flowing from him toward you, feeling your hearts melting together. Breathe for a few minutes more and then let him go, thanking him for the forgiveness that he's offering you, allowing yourself to feel the forgiveness flowing from him to you. Be aware of yourself again, breathing in through your nose and out through your mouth, breathing slowly and deeply, feeling yourself present, here and now, relaxing with each breath.

Step 3. Now allow an image of yourself to come to you. Imagine you are sitting in a chair across from yourself. Look at yourself and say, *"I forgive you for whatever you feel you've done to hurt yourself, for however you've let yourself down. I forgive you."* Feel the sensation of opening your heart to yourself, feeling the connection between you and the image of yourself sitting in the chair across from you. Allow the sensation of opening and softening to pass from you to your image, and from your image back to you, uniting you. Breathe in and out, staying soft, relaxing, feeling forgiveness, for a few moments more.

Step 4 - Allow the feeling of forgiveness to spread from you and your heart to all those on the planet who are in need of forgiveness. Allow this feeling to grow and expand, breathing in and out, relaxing for a few minutes. Let that image fade. Be aware of yourself again, breathing in through your nose and out through your mouth, breathing slowly and deeply, feeling yourself present here and now, relaxing. When you're ready, open your eyes and bring your attention back into the room.

CHAPTER 18
PURPOSE
"HAVE SOMETHING TO DO"

*"The mystery of human existence lies not in just staying alive,
but in finding something to live for."*
—Fyodor Dostoyevsky

Each of us has a purpose in this life, but when we are going
through change, we often lose sense of what that is. We each have
something divine within us that is meant to interact with the universe in some way, and whatever experiences we go through help
us develop into who we are meant to be.

In the ancient Chinese meditations of Yoga and Qi Gong, we
begin by saying "Namaste," a gesture to send positivity to the
universe in hopes of receiving it back. When we say it to each,
other it means the divine in me recognizes the divine in you. Recognizing our divine nature gives our lives meaning, whether or
not things seem to be going our way. When we have lost someone
or something, it is easy to wonder what meaning our own life has.
When we keep trying over and over again to make a change and
make little or no progress, we sometimes may wonder, "What's
the point?"

It is in living our lives the best we can, no matter what the
circumstances, that we find meaning. We may not do anything
grandiose, and it may not seem as though what we do really matters, but as George realizes at the end of the movie *It's a Wonderful Life,* his life matters and has meaning. When all seems to
be lost, or we feel stuck, our life may seem trivial as we do the
same things over and over, whether it is staying at home taking

care of children or loved ones or going to a humdrum job. Just getting up every day and having something to do is essential to happiness. Even if it's something we don't particularly like, it can lead us to finding our purpose. The following are a few short examples of this:

Kelly dreamed of being a dancer or actress. When that didn't happen for her, she became depressed and found solace in partying with her friends. She held a few jobs here and there but would eventually lose them due to late nights out causing her to miss work. She went from job to job feeling unfulfilled and finding herself using more and more substances to fill that void.

That was until she made a drastic change in her life, moving to a new state and taking a job in a nursing home. While she didn't make as much money as at some of her other jobs, she found that helping people gave her a sense of purpose. This job led her to pursuing a nursing degree.

Chan came from Vietnam as a child and felt pressure from her parents to excel in school. She worked hard and was in the pre-med program in college. She got very involved in everything: she volunteered, shadowed doctors, became the president of the pre-med club, and minored in anthropology. She wanted to help people and felt medicine was the way she could do that, but after graduation she wasn't happy and no longer felt it was the right career path for her.

For the next seven years, Chan worked in various jobs trying to figure out what she wanted to do with her life. She continued searching for her purpose until one day she came across the master's degree program in social work and thought, *This is what I've been looking for!* Social work gives her the opportunity to help people in a way that is more meaningful to her than medicine. She learned how good it feels to talk to people who need her and how caring and flexible she can be compared to how she once was. She is passionate about working with the elderly and feels this is what she is meant to do.

Knowing that your life has meaning and that there is a purpose for your existence brings a sense of fulfillment and happiness. That purpose must be good for something beyond you. Living our purpose while embracing resilience through change will bring a perspective that honors our uniqueness. Seeing meaning in our life requires us to develop a view of our life in which we can see our own worth.

By seeing our worth, we can feel better about the things we do, whether they are large or small. A sense of purpose helps us prioritize our lives and helps us to be happy, even while working in a job we don't like or doing mundane daily tasks. A sense of purpose not only helps us to find and do things that add meaning to our life, but also helps when things go wrong, when life presents unforeseen events like sickness or accidents, or when we might not achieve what we strive for. It helps us put those events in perspective, to refocus on the things that are meaningful, and to move ahead and enjoy life. Research shows that people who find their purpose are open to change in their lives. They tend to challenge themselves and battle against their fears. Challenging yourself regularly and pursuing things that reinforce a sense of purpose, meaning, and accomplishment increase serotonin.

Not only will finding your purpose increase your happiness, but an added benefit is that you will have better physical health. There's research that links feelings of having a sense of purpose to positive health outcomes such as fewer strokes and heart attacks, better sleep, and a lower risk of dementia and disabilities.

You may be thinking, *"But how do I find my purpose?"* Self-reflection, listening to others, finding where your passions lay, and simply thinking about what you love to do is a great start. It's nice when your purpose lines up with your work, but often it doesn't, so notice what you think about most of the time or what things you feel good about when you are doing them. For example, health and wellness are something I have been interested in since I was a teenager, but it wasn't until I worked with my clients and had my own health issues that I studied and researched to learn more about how to better my life and those around me.

Few people know what their purpose is from an early age. More often than not, finding your purpose can be a lifelong journey, and it can change over time as you evolve. One client loved biology and became a veterinarian only to find out later in life the benefits of honey and her passion for bees. She continues to have a career as a veterinarian, but she finds her fulfillment and purpose in working with bees. Going through life's challenges can often help us find our purpose. Many people who have suffered with addiction find purpose in helping others as a sponsor or group facilitator. The changes and difficulties we go through can help us find our purpose in life and how we can best help others and feel fulfilled and happy.

GUIDE

1. Write down your own mission statement or purpose. Some examples might be being a positive influence in the lives of others, teaching and inspiring children to learn and know they can succeed, or bringing beauty to the world through art or music.

Start by meditating or praying daily to find your divine purpose, or take time to think about when you feel good about yourself. *"Is it when I am creating a piece of art, decorating my home, finding bargains, volunteering, working with animals, or cleaning the environment?"*

Think about topics you regularly talk about with friends, family or on social media. Take a look at pictures you post and see if there is a particular activity you are doing over and over like music, art, gardening, hiking, cooking, or volunteering. Your closest friends and family may have some insight, so reach out to them and ask them what they notice about you and what you're passionate about. Notice when someone pays you a compliment or makes an observation about you and look for patterns.

2. Do something that is meaningful for you, whether it's your job or another activity. Volunteer at a church, community center, homeless shelter, animal shelter, or nature center. Get involved in a cause like running, walking, funding, or research for breast cancer, diabetes, etc. Write a book, poem, or article, even if it's just for your own pleasure. Our lives have meaning and sharing our stories can help others through difficult times.

CHAPTER 19
SELF-CARE
"TAKE CARE OF YOU"

"Happiness is not something you postpone for the future; it is something you design for the present"—Jim Rohn

When we are preoccupied with changes that disrupt our lives, the last thing we think about is our own self-care. Often, we are so overwhelmed, distraught, stressed, or anxious that all we can think about is the problem or circumstance in which we find ourselves. I saw this with my mother, who was so busy taking care of seven children and putting their needs above her own that it eventually took a serious toll on her health. She ended up gaining a lot of weight, which then resulted in several back surgeries and two knee replacements. It has taken her years to realize the importance of self-care, but she now takes the time to exercise daily and eat better which resulted in losing 35 pounds. She treats herself to manicures and reading novels for enjoyment.

Doing these little things keeps her healthy as she continues to serve her family and others on a daily basis. Self-care is any activity that we do deliberately in order to take care of our mental, emotional, and physical health. It is key to improving mood and reducing anxiety. It's also key to a good relationship with oneself and others. If we don't take enough care of ourselves, we won't be in a position to give to our loved ones either. Self-care is something that refuels us, rather than takes from us.

You might consider a lazy day sitting around, watching TV is self-care, but our bodies were meant to move, so even if you need a relaxing day, include some type of physical movement too. Exercise is one of the best forms of self-care you can do because it releases endorphins that trigger a positive feeling in your body, and you develop a more positive and energizing outlook on life. It also increases serotonin levels, leading to improved mood and energy. Eating a nutritious healthy diet, exercising, getting enough sleep, practicing meditation, getting a massage, manicure or pedicure, and spending time with friends or loved ones are all acts of self-care. Many of these increase endorphins, serotonin, dopamine, and oxytocin. They don't require a lot of effort. If you've done the guided activities in this book you've already started practicing self-care.

When we look at some examples of people who have gone through the most difficult times of change with a positive outlook, we notice that they all had self-care in common. For example: Bob still takes time to exercise daily, create art sculptures, and spend time with his wife and family. Spencer took time to exercise, be with friends, and play basketball after his wife died. Erica took time to go out with friends and to go on mini daily exercise dates with Spencer. Chris took time to run, golf, and enjoy his family, and even now as he goes through chemo once again, he continues to walk daily. Irene takes time to write, garden, paint, and visit her grandchildren.

Doing little things like going for a walk, doing a few breathing or yoga poses, going to lunch with a friend, getting a massage, getting a pedicure, or even just sitting outside enjoying nature can all be rejuvenating acts of self-care.

GUIDE

Write down things you like to do

Examples: Paint, dance, play the piano, play guitar, practice tennis, run, ski, go to the beach, see movies, visit a nature park, play board games, read, walk, talk with friends, bike, rollerblade, work out, sing karaoke, waterski, jet-ski, golf, fish.

_____

_____

_____

_____

_____

_____

_____

_____

_____

_____

_____

_____

Take at least twenty minutes every day to practice self-care. It can be the same thing every day or something different,.just so long as you have at least one thing to look forward to every day. It can be as simple as taking a walk or spending twenty minutes unwinding.

Look for opportunities to laugh! This raises endorphins. Read the comics or look at funny videos or memes.

CHAPTER 20
QUALITY RELATIONSHIPS

"Good relationships keep us happier and healthier. Period!"
—Robert Waldinger

Sometimes when we are going through a change, we want to be alone and isolate ourselves from the world. Perhaps we feel we can get through things on our own, we're embarrassed or don't want to burden other people with our problems. There is a difference between needing a little time alone and isolating. Time alone can give us the opportunity to meditate and process change, whereas isolation can lead to feelings of loneliness, depression, negative self-esteem, and other mental health problems.

When we have people we can call upon to help us through change, we recognize we are not alone ,and our burden is lighter. Two researchers out of Virginia found that if you're looking at a hill you need to climb by yourself, your brain shows you a hill that is twenty percent steeper than if you look at the same hill with someone who is going to climb the hill with you. The geometry of challenges in your life are constantly in flux based upon whether you think you're alone or with other people with whom to overcome a challenge. According to the eighty-year Harvard study, the greatest predictor of long-term happiness is our connection with others, and loneliness is as deadly as smoking or alcoholism.

Our human nature is such that we are designed to connect. Think about what makes you happy, like falling in love, hanging out with friends, visiting your parents, children and grandchildren. Remember, that oxytocin is released with physical touch

167

and close relationships, so when you give each other a hug, pick up a child, or even stroke your dog or cat, you increase oxytocin. Unfortunately with social media on the rise, personal social interaction has gone down, and loneliness has gone up. Researchers have warned that loneliness and social isolation are more dangerous than obesity and can be as damaging to health as smoking fifteen cigarettes a day. The good news is that increasing quality relationships can reduce these risks and can even speed recovery of illness.

Going through difficulties like the death of a child or a severe illness to one or both partners can take a toll on any relationship, especially marriage. Since my own marriage ended after twenty-eight years, I've had a special interest in researching and observing long-lasting happy marriages in hopes of helping others.

There are two key ingredients to quality relationships which relationship experts have noted. The first is **trust**. Whether it's your spouse, partner or friend, trust is essential. Knowing that that person will be there no matter what. The second is **respect.** Studies show that even though a couple bickers or one partner nags another, if they still admire and respect each other they enjoy a lasting relationship.

You may recall Bob and Phyllis from earlier. Even when Phyllis was completely nonfunctional after the death of their daughter, Bob respected her for who she was and knew he wanted to be with her no matter what. She knew she could count on him during that time and he on her when he had his kidney transplant. Even when Phyllis is on Bob's case to drink water, exercise, and eat well, or he jokingly complains how she is the boss, they both speak highly of each other, saying things like, *"He's the best, one of a kind,"* or, *"There's no one like Phyllis."* The same was evident with Chris when he described his wife as *"a rockstar."* and with Spencer when he said, *"Erica is amazing, patient, humble, bright, and has an optimistic outlook."*

Quality relationships can be developed even when a partner or loved one has passed. Having worked with older populations for the past twenty-five years, I have witnessed those who have lost a partner and have then found happiness in their friendships. They find new friendships as they participate in activities like fitness classes, book clubs, canasta, mahjong, bunko, cards or other groups. One woman who lost her husband found a close network of friends in her fitness class. Having people you can count on is key to happiness.

During the COVID quarantine of 2020, this was apparent as I witnessed several groups meet virtually, often several times a week. One group of friends who had met in college and recently graduated called each other and did a FaceTime chat every evening just to check in and see how everyone's day was. They shared everything from stress, anxiety and depression from being isolated to how their plants were growing or how work was, problems with family or how they were struggling with eating healthy and exercising. They listened, empathized, and gave each other encouragement and support. They have respect and admiration for each other even though they come from very different backgrounds, are different ages, and have very distinct personalities. They recognize the strengths each other has and they accept and appreciate each other just for who they are. Their friendship is closer now than ever before.

Many of the clients I worked with in a residential addiction center did not have friends and didn't know how to build quality friendships. Those who isolated themselves almost always relapsed within a month. Those who learned to cultivate relationships were not only happier but had fewer relapses. One woman upon leaving the center joined a local church group and invited a couple of her friends to come with her. Their friendship grew as they attended church sponsored activities together and supported each other in their recovery. They now have each other to rely on and can call whenever they need to. They are not only all still sober but also much happier as their friendship flourishes.

Research shows that happy people spend more time with others and have a richer set of social connections than unhappy people. Studies show that the simple act of talking to a stranger on the street can boost our mood more than we expect. The importance of others cannot be overstated in challenging times, because our instinctive tendencies push us toward the opposite. We're wired to close down in shame when we struggle. We're wired to unite in smaller and more competitive tribes of "us" versus "them" when we feel threatened. We see it both in our politics and in our personal lives, which are becoming increasingly dependent on virtual friends and online forums. Yet, research shows that human touch is one of our most basic needs. A smile, a touch, or someone who listens and understands can regulate the sympathetic nervous system, return us to a state of calm, and ignite our own compassion so we can extend it to others.

GUIDE

1. **Make one new social connection weekly.** It can be a small five-minute act like sparking a conversation with someone on public transportation, asking a coworker about his/her day, or chatting with someone in line at a coffee shop.

2. **Develop a strong network that you can readily call on.** At least once this week, take a whole hour to connect with someone you care about. The key is that you must take the time needed to genuinely connect with another person. At the end of the day, list the social connection you made and notice how you feel when you write it down.

3. List three people you can call when going through a challenge.

_____

_____

_____

"It doesn't matter what we're doing, just being together is what makes us happy."

CHAPTER 21
SOMETHING TO LOOK
FORWARD TO

"Our drive to look ahead needn't cause a permanent state of dissatisfaction, as seeking is itself a fulfilling activity."

When we are going through a change, it is hard to think about anything else. Looking forward to better times can help us get through the hard times. One of our core instincts is to seek, so when we are in pain, we seek relief. Focusing on the pain will only increase the pain but focusing on things we look forward to doing helps us feel happier. Sometimes that can be difficult when the challenge is so daunting, but knowing that there is a future to look forward to beyond the challenge can help. For example, one family who lost their daughter could look forward to the birth of their first grandchild.

This didn't take away their loss, but it made life a little easier knowing that there were still things they could look forward to even in their pain. Remembering the things you look forward to doing, seeing, or being is essential in moving forward in change. For example, if you are struggling with health challenges, looking forward to feeling better and being able to do those things you want, will help you endure through that time. For those who find themselves single after many years of marriage due to divorce or death of a spouse, redefining their "bucket list" and what things they look forward to may look different than what they had thought. Many have found joy in unexpected adventures and endeavors and are doing things they never imagined.

For example, after the death of her husband, one woman decided to take each of her kids individually on a trip with her. She looks forward to spending one-on-one time with them that she would never have had the opportunity to do before.

Another woman had a dream of being an artist, so after her divorce she took several classes and eventually started her own business selling her paintings online and in art shows.

Going back to school was something I never thought I would do, but after my divorce I had a newfound desire to learn and seek out as much knowledge as I possibly could. Even after graduating I continue to seek opportunities to learn new things by watching Ted Talks, reading books, and listening to podcasts. I look forward to going on ski trips and vacations I had only dreamt about before.

One key to finding happiness lies in our enjoyment of the journey as we seek it. If we think we're going to be happy once we achieve something or get to where we want to be, we're denying ourselves that happiness-inducing state of constantly seeking. So, learn a new language or skill, build your intelligence and exercise your brain, explore new countries and regions, or just learn more about people and the world around you. Thomas Jefferson was quite insightful when he wrote, *"We have the right to the pursuit of happiness,"* rather than implying that we have the right to be happy.

Remember that dopamine is increased when we anticipate or have something to look forward to. It is our striving emotion, so having something to look forward to increases the level of dopamine in the brain, which makes us happier. No matter what your circumstances, you can always have something to look forward to. Larry is an example of someone, who even after being paralyzed, was still able to find things to look forward to.

Larry's Story

Larry's life changed drastically from one day to the next. Following the best golf day of his life, he went to his high school reunion. The very next day he woke up and couldn't move. He was paralyzed from the neck down due to contracting the West Nile Virus.

Eventually, movement in his upper body returned, and he regained use of his arms. I was impressed by Larry's desire to build his strength and to add more exercise than the physical therapy he was receiving.

Larry's attitude was such an inspiration to me that I wondered what it was that made Larry cheerful. He told me that he and his wife have a cabin they love to go to, so they were building accommodations for his wheelchair. He looks forward to spending several months of the year there enjoying nature and being together with his family.

While he can no longer golf, he looks forward to watching golf tournaments as well as other informative shows and documentaries on T.V. His life is not what he expected, but he continues to learn and share his knowledge with others. He always had something interesting to share with me during our training sessions.

We can learn a great lesson from Larry not to let our circumstances— no matter how difficult or life shattering they might be— to get in the way of finding things to look forward to and enjoy in life. Life does not always turn out how we expect, and even when it does, neuroscience has found happiness comes from continually seeking. One study concluded that the real key to happiness is in realizing that attaining any or all of those things we think we really, really want will never actually make us happy.

As you go through change, remember that the challenges and negative experiences you have will enable you to feel a greater sense of happiness!

"Enjoy the pursuit to happiness!"

GUIDE

Write a list of things you look forward to doing.

What are things you have wanted to do or learn? Perhaps playing tennis, salsa dancing, painting, playing an instrument, or learning a language or other skill? Strive to build your intelligence and exercise your brain. Explore new countries and regions; make it a goal to learn more about the world around you. Challenge yourself and enjoy the challenge!

_____

_____

_____

_____

_____

_____

_____

_____

_____

_____

_____

_____

"There is no way to happiness, happiness is the way."
—Lao Tzu

EPILOGUE

"The purpose of life is to be happy."
—Dalai Lama

We will all experience unwanted and wanted change throughout our lives. When we choose to find meaning in an experience and look for the benefits, we can be happy. One of my favorite quotes is by the author Og Mandino, who said,

> *"Search for the seed of good in adversity. Master that principle and you will own a precious shield that will guard you well through all the darkest valleys you must traverse. Stars may be seen from the bottom of a deep well, when they cannot be discerned from the mountain top. So will you learn things in adversity that you would never have discovered without trouble. There is always a seed of good. Find it and prosper."*

Our own personal definition of happiness may change over time as we go through change and experience life. It is my personal view that we exist to be happy and to help others be happy. We can be happy knowing that at the very least, we have persevered and developed the ability to empathize and comfort others because of our experience. It is my hope that as you have read and followed the guides in this book, you have been inspired to find hope, health, and happiness through whatever change you are experiencing.

"Happiness is the meaning and the purpose of life, the whole aim and end of human existence."—Aristotle

179

Acknowledgements

I am thankful for people who were put in my life at the right time and place to inspire, lift, and help me. Some will never know the influence they've had on me and others. I believe we are all exactly where we need to be to learn and help each other on our life's journey.

A special thanks to all those who took the time to share their stories and have trusted me to share them with you. All of the experiences shared are from people I've personally known or worked with over the past thirty-six years. Most of the names have been changed except for a few whom I specifically interviewed for this book.

Thanks to my family and friends who have supported and listened to me as I read and reread excerpts. A special acknowledgment to my social work friends, who over the course of my writing this, patiently listened, contributed, and encouraged me to keep writing.

Thanks to my mentor, Dale Christensen, who gave me the confidence boost and nudge I needed to publish this book.

Lastly, thanks to a great team of editors who helped me bring this to you.

Selected Sources

Introduction

A.Cipriani, T. A. Furukawa, G. Salanti, A. Chaimani, L. Z Atkinson, Y. Ogawa, S. Leucht, H. G Ruhe, E.H. Turner, J. P. T. Higgins, *et al.*(2018) Comparative efficacy and acceptability of 21 antidepressant drugs for the acute treatment of adults with major depressive disorder: a systematic review and network meta-analysis, Lancet, http://dx.doi.org/10.1016/ S0140-6736(17)32802-7

B. L. Smith, June 2012, Inappropriate prescribing of America, *American Psychological*, Vol 43, No. 6, p 6

Part One - Change

C.C. DiClemente, J.O. Prochaska (1985) Processes and stages of change: coping and competence in smoking behavior change. American Journal of Health Behavior, 25, 217-227

W.R. Miller, S. Rollinick, (2002) Motivational Interviewing, Preparing People for Change, The Guilford Press Inc, New York, NY, Chapter 15

K. A. Baikie, & K. Wilhelm, (2005). Emotional and physical health benefits of expressive writing. *Advances in Psychiatric Treatment 11*, 338-346. doi:10.1192/apt.11.5.338

R. Howes, (2011). Journaling in therapy. *Psychology Today.* Retrieved from https://www.psychologytoday.com/blog/in-therapy/201101/journaling-in-therapy Murray, B. (2002). *Writing to heal.* Monitor. Retrieved from http://www.apa.org/monitor/jun02/writing.aspx

J. M. Smyth, A. A. Stone, A. Hurewitz, & A. Kaell, (1999). Effects of writing about stressful experiences on symptom reduction in patients with asthma or rheumatoid arthritis: A randomized trial. *Journal of the American Medical Association 281*, 1304-1309.

M. Tartakovsky, (2015). The power of writing: 3 types of therapeutic writing. *Psych Central.* Retrieved from types-of-therapeutic-writing/

Michael K. Scullin et as. "The Effects of Bedtime Writing on Difficult Falling Asleep: A Polysomnographic Study Comparing To-Do Lists and Completed Activity Lists." Journal of Experimental Psychology: General 2018, Vol. 147, No. 1, 139-146

A. S. Froerer, J. B. Cziffra-Bergs, J. S. Kim, and E. E. Connie, (2018) Solution Focused Brief Therapy with Clients Managing Trauma, Oxford University Press, pp 105,173,184

E. Jones-Smith, (2014) Strengths-Based Therapy: Connecting Theory, Practice and Skills. SAGE Publications.

Charles Duhigg, 2012, The Power of Habit, Random House, New York, NY.

Part Two – Hope

Peterson & Seligman., (2004). Character Strengths & Virtues: A Handbook And
Classification. New York: American Psychological Association & Oxford
University Press. J. K. Staples, J. A. Atti, J. A., & J. S. Gordon, (2011).
Mind-body skills groups for post-traumatic stress disorder and depression
symptoms in Palestinian children and adolescents in Gaza. *International
Journal of Stress Management, 18*(3), 246-262. Doi:10.1037/a0024015

Idler, Ellen, John Blevins, Mimi Kiser, and Carol Hogue. 2017. "Religion, a social
determinant of mortality? A 10-year follow-up of the Health and
Retirement Study PLoS One. J. Gordon, 2009 Unstuck pg. 298, 407

Green, L. S., Oades, L. G., & Grant, A. M. (2006). Cognitive-behavioral, solution-
focused life coaching: Enhancing goal striving, well-being, and
hope. *The Journal of Positive Psychology, 1*(3), 142–149. doi:
10.1080/17439760600619849 (Mind mapping is an effective
intervention also used to increase hope and optimism. A research
study done on solution-focused life coaching showed that this can
increases goal striving and hope, in addition to overall well-being.)

Part Three – Mind-Body Connection

D. M. Davis, J.A. Hayes, (2012), What are the benefits of Mindfulness, *Monitor on
Psychology,* Vol 43, No. 7, Print version: p 64

J. K. Staples, J. A. Atti, J. A., & J. S. Gordon, (2011). Mind-body skills groups for
post-traumatic stress disorder and depression symptoms in Palestinian children and adolescents in Gaza. *International Journal of Stress Management,
18*(3), 246-262. Doi:10.1037/a0024015

www.Sane.org, (2018) *Antidepressant Medication,* Vol May 10

James S. Gordon, 2008, Unstuck, Penguin group, New York, NY

Part Four - Health

www.Sane.org, (2018) *Antidepressant Medication,* Vol May 10

Thomas, D. M., Bouchard, C., Church, T., Slentz, C., Kraus, W. E., Redman, L. M.,
Martin, C. K., Silva, A. M., Vossen, M., Westerterp, K., & Heymsfield, S.
B. (2012). Why do individuals not lose more weight from an exercise intervention at a defined dose? An energy balance analysis. *Obesity reviews: an
official journal of the International Association for the Study of Obesity, 13*(10), 835–847. https://doi.org/10.1111/j.1467-789X.2012.01012.x

Y. Chen, Y. Cui, S. Chen, Z. Wu, (2017) Relationship between sleep and muscle
strength among Chinese university students: a cross-sectional
study. *Journal of musculoskeletal & neuronal interactions, 17*(4), 327–333.

N. Buchmann, D. Spira, K.Norman, I. Demuth, R. Eckardt,, E. Steinhagen-Thiessen,
(2016). Sleep, Muscle Mass and Muscle Function in Older People. *Deutsches Arzte-
blatt international, 113*(15), 253–260 https://doi.org/10.3238/arztebl.2016.0253

K. Michael, Scullin et as. "The Effects of Bedtime Writing on Difficult Falling Asleep: A Polysomnographic Study Comparing To-Do Lists and Completed Activity Lists." Journal of Experimental Psychology: General 2018, Vol. 147, No. 1, 139-146

M. Emoto, 2008, The Healing Power of Water, Hay House Inc, Carlsbad, CA

E. Selhub, Nutritional psychiatry: Your brain on food, Harvard Health Publishing, March 26

A.M. Waggas (2009). Neuroprotective evaluation of extract of ginger (Zingiber officinale) root in monosodium glutamate-induced toxicity in different brain areas male albino rats. *Pakistan journal of biological sciences: PJBS, 12*(3), 201–212. https://doi.org/10.3923/pjbs.2009.201.212

H. G. Ağalar, (2019) Nonvitamin and Nonmineral Nutritional Supplements

J. Sanmukhani, A. Anovadiya, et al. (2011) Evaluation of antidepressant like activity of curcumin and its combination with fluoxetine and imipramine: an acute and chronic study. *Acta Ppol Pharm.* Sep-Oct:68 (5):769-75

S. Kulkarni, A. Dhir, et al. (2009) Potentials of curcumin as an antidepressant. *Scientific World-Journal.* Nov 1;9: 1233-41.

S. Kulkarni, M.K. Bhutani, et al. (2009) Antidepressant activity of curcumin: involvement of serotonin and dopamine system. *Psychopharmacology (Berl).* Dec; 201 (3): 435-42. Epub 2008 Sep. 3.

A. Zampelas, D. B. Panagiotakos, C. Pitsavos, C. Chrysohoou, C. Stefanadis, (2004) Associations between Coffee Consumption and Inflammatory Markers in Healthy persons: the ATTICA study, *The American Journal of Clinical Nutrition*, Volume 80, Issue 4, October 2004, Pages 862–867, https://doi.org/10.1093/ajcn/80.4.862

Part Five - Happiness

D.Duggal, A. Sacks-Zimmerman, and T. Liberta (2016). The Impact of Hope and Resilience on Multiple Factors in Neurosurgical Patients, Cureus. 2016 Oct; 8(10): e849.

D. Berendes,, F. J. Keefe, T. J. Somers, S M. Kothadia., L. S. Porter, J.S. Cheavens, (2010). Hope in the context of lung cancer: relationships of hope to symptoms and psychological distress. *Journal of pain and symptom management, 40*(2), 174–182. https://doi.org/10.1016/j.jpainsymman.2010.01.014

R. Carlson, 1992, You Can be Happy No Matter What, MJF Publishing, New York,

D. Gilbert, 2005, Stumbling on Happiness, Random House Inc. New York.

D. Buettner, 2006, The Blue Zones of Happiness, National Geographic Partners, LLC, Washington D.C.

J. S. Gordon, 2008, Unstuck, Penguin group, New York, NY

ABOUT THE AUTHOR
Kendra Crompton

Kendra Crompton founded Life Change Solutions LLC in 2019 integrating her experience in fitness and nutrition with her mental health training to help others as they go through life changes. She has a master's degree in Social Work and an undergraduate degree in Communications, to which she has added numerous certifications and clinical experience.

With over 36 years of experience in the health and fitness industry as a personal trainer and holistic health consultant she is a trusted mentor, consultant, life coach, seminar facilitator and motivational speaker.

Kendra specializes in working with people through past and present trauma, addiction, emotional challenges and mental issues such as anxiety, stress and depression. She has a keen sense and understanding that allows her to connect with, inspire and motivate her clients.

Her solution-focused consultation style assists clients through challenges while guiding them on their path to achieve their objectives, maximize their potential and find hope, health and happiness along the way.

You can reach the author by contacting her at: **mylifechangesolutions.com,** https://linkedin.com/in/kendra-crompton-7692a013/

NOTE: Go to Amazon.com and author Kendra Crompton to find other books in the series and by this author. Use the "Other Options" all for international shipping.

Printed in Great Britain
by Amazon

23315218R00106